THE MR PORTER PAPERBACK

# THE MR PORTER PAPER-BACK

THE MANUAL FOR
A STYLISH
LIFE

VOLUME ONE

Thames & Hudson

Published in 2013 in paperback in the United States of America
by Thames & Hudson Inc., 500 Fifth Avenue, New York,
New York 10110

*thamesandhudsonusa.com*

Library of Congress Catalog Card Number 2013941441

ISBN 978-0-500-29126-9

Printed in China

# CONTENTS

# FOREWORD

WELCOME to this inky incarnation of MR PORTER. We hope you enjoy our collection of interviews, advice columns, insider tips, recommendations and style commentaries plucked from the weekly content published throughout the year on our website.

Why a print version? Because we like to be at your beck and call wherever you are, whatever time it is, whatever mood you're in – whether it's at the touch of a button, or the turn of a page.

I hope that each time you dip in and out of this paperback you will not only feel more informed, but more inspired. Style has never been so wholly embraced by a generation of men as it is now: there are no fashion diktats anymore, no trends you have to follow; today, it's just about feeling good, looking your best (because you want to), and enjoying every moment of it. We all work hard, we all read bleak things in the news, we all worry about our futures, so why not embrace the things in our lives that make us smile, or feel confident about ourselves? They're important, and you know what, we deserve them.

Mr Jeremy Langmead
Editor-in-Chief

"Clothes make the man. Naked people have little or no influence on society"

Mr Mark Twain

## THE LOOK

# MR TINIE TEMPAH

*Talent, style and charm: Alex Bilmes, editor of British* Esquire,
*meets the rapper making his mark on music and British menswear*

TWO WEEKS BEFORE my interview with Mr Tinie Tempah I happened to spend an afternoon at Soho House West Hollywood, in a penthouse 14 floors above Sunset Boulevard. Mr Hugh Laurie was there, eating *en famille*. Cross-legged on the floor, taking her lunch from a coffee table, was the aggressively kooky sitcom star Ms Zooey Deschanel. The actress Ms Elizabeth Banks was in the bar, as was the director and screenwriter Mr Paul Haggis. It's that kind of place: quinoa salad, sunglasses, box-office goss. And there, in a corner, as chilled as my Pellegrino, was Mr Tempah, the British rapper – remember when that job title was oxymoronic? – whose hit song, "Written in the Stars", has sold millions of singles in the US. Suffice to say MC Tunes never came so far, or climbed so high.

The next time I see Mr Tempah he's standing on a mantelpiece in a high-ceilinged central London townhouse, having his photo taken for MR PORTER. The Smiths' "This Charming Man" is playing, which is appropriate to our subject insofar as he is extremely personable, but inappropriate in that when he inevitably does go out tonight, he will have more than a stitch to wear. There's the shark-print T-shirt he keeps on for our conversation, for starters. "It's good to do a photoshoot occasionally," he proclaims. "It helps keep you up to date on trends." Yes, I tell him, I find that too. If I don't pose for a fashion shoot now and then, I feel so out of the designer label loop. Mr Tempah giggles. I told you he was a charmer.

So what was he doing in LA? *Jay Leno*, of course. It was his third time on the show. (Mr Tempah can report that Mr Leno does a better class of goodie bag.) But he's there all the time. "It's like a second home," he says, with the nonchalance of the club-class nomad.

The most exciting British male solo artist in years (we're good at girls, but of late the boys have been tiresomely insipid), Mr Tempah, real name Mr Patrick Chukwuemeka Okogwu, has the potential to overhaul his contemporaries and collaborators – Messrs Dizzee Rascal, Tinchy Stryder, Labrinth – to become the biggest UK rapper to date, the man with the most universal and international pop appeal. He knows it, he appreciates it, he's excited by it, but he doesn't feel overawed at all.

"Every couple of days I have a pinch-myself moment," he says, "but I've decided to just embrace it. This is one of those once-in-a-lifetime chances and you can't be walking around overwhelmed all the time. You're never going to get anything done if you're always flustered. And I'm quite good at adapting to situations."

A product of the less than salubrious streets of southeast London – Mr Tempah lived on a famously tough estate in Peckham until, when he was 12, the family relocated to slightly leafier Plumstead – he is the son of striving Nigerian parents who arrived in England in their twenties and instilled, he says, a serious work ethic in the eldest of their four kids.

"It was about discipline in everything you do," he says. "I was always told that because I am of Nigerian heritage I'd have to work 10 times harder. You take a bit of what you want from [what you're told as a child], and you get rid of the rest, but I really believed that, and you've got nothing to lose if you believe that. If you work 10 times as hard as anyone else, you're going to do well."

The Nigerian background, he says, might also explain the desire to look sharp. It's not the case, he says, that Mr Tempah is always suited and booted, but whether he's in Savile Row or sneakers – or

Savile Row *and* sneakers – he does like to look his best. "Being Nigerian we like opulence," he says. "If you go to any Nigerian home you'll see red carpets, leather sofas, china plates. And the influence of the British, because Nigeria was a colony: speaking properly, behaving a certain way, making sure your tie is straight, your cuffs and your collars are clean."

As for the modest background, that was inspiring rather than frustrating. "I was that kid in Peckham living opposite those two-million-pound houses," he says. "I could see that family with the 2.4 children and the Range Rover and the dog from my tower block. From as young as I can remember I was like, 'Mum, how come we live up here and they live down there? What did they have to do to get that house? Why do they have a driveway and we have to go into a lift?'" One of the great advantages of London, he says, is the proximity of great wealth to those less fortunate. "If you don't see those things, if they don't become real to you, then you don't believe it's possible and that makes it a lot more difficult to attain."

Mr Tempah could have gone on to university but at 16 he was performing in clubs and experimenting with making music at home, and he knew he had an entrepreneurial streak. By 19 he had made a name for himself on London's grime scene, and was releasing music on his own label – and now multi-purpose brand – Disturbing London. In 2009 he signed to Parlophone, home to leading British artists including Coldplay, Blur and The Chemical Brothers. He was still living at home with his parents but he was about to conquer mainstream UK pop.

In February 2010 his first single, an irrepressible paean to hedonism called "Pass Out", went straight to No.1. When his mother called from work to congratulate him on the news, she didn't neglect to mention that there was a congestion charge letter downstairs that needed his attention. "That's how real it was," he says. Three months later he was supporting Rihanna on tour and in June of that year he performed "Pass Out" with Snoop Dogg on Glastonbury's Pyramid

Stage. *Disc-Overy*, his debut album, went to No.1. The boisterous sound of a young man having a seriously good time, it showcased his shuffle-style skipping of genres, fusing hip-hop, grime, drum'n'bass, house and pop with witty lyrics and a heavy dose of bathos to offset the braggadocio. Mr Tempah was, he announced, "about to be a bigger star than my mum thought". Then there was the fact that "I've got so many clothes I keep some at my aunt's house." In 2011 he won Brit Awards for Best Single, for "Pass Out", and Best Breakthrough Act.

It's his exploding of the stereotype of the angrily boastful rapper, he thinks, that has endeared him to the public. "There's humour in my music," he says. "I'm a safe, friendly way for people to embrace hip-hop. It's not all about how many people you've shot and stabbed and killed or how much money you've got." And even though he now has his own place to keep his clothes in, as well, one imagines, as girls and cash on tap – Mr Tempah doesn't dispute this point when I mention it – he doesn't feel he's lost touch with his USP: the people's rapper. "When I come off tour I go to Asda," he says. "I clean my house. I do the ironing."

His second album, *Demonstration*, is, he says, the product of his ongoing musical education, of touring the world, taking advice from new friends including Messrs Chris Martin and Damon Albarn. "It's very loud and hard and heavy," he says, "and there are some very beautiful moments. It's very personal. I felt a duty to let people in a bit more. I'm living the dream, it's a hell of a ride and I just want to let people know what is going on in my life."

One of the things going on is a developing interest in clothes. He started really caring about the way he dresses, he says, when he began to perform live in his teens. "I knew then that I can't be wearing the same Nike sweats as the guy in the crowd. It's show biz, you've got to make it a little more premium."

He's often pegged as the latest example of the straightforward English dandy, but that's another stereotype he's keen to subvert.

His style is more nuanced. It has grown out of hip-hop's sportswear label fetish, the tradition of London football casuals, his visits to hipster style capitals such as Stockholm, as well as a respect for the traditions of British tailoring. Eventually, out of all those influences, he says, "you find you've got your own little thing going on".

In fact, so influential is his look – the thick-rimmed Harry Palmer specs, the natty bow ties, the box-fresh sneakers – that he is on the committee for London Collections: Men, the three-day British menswear showcase that takes place twice a year. It's hard to think of a more appropriate representative for the best of British men's style, his tastes at once cutting-edge contemporary and fogeyishly traditional. "I feel as if London is so popular right now," he says. "So much great talent is here. This is the place. It's the epicentre of a lot of cool." Then, in pleasingly Mr Tempah fashion, he brings us back to earth.

"Right, let's get out of these damn clothes."

THE REPORT

# SMART WORKERS

*From the coolest of clocks to the sharpest of desk sets,
we show you the best-designed accessories
for a winning work space*

THERE'S SOMETHING REASSURING about a man sitting behind
a solid wood desk, leaning on a leather writing mat with notes of
beeswax circulating around him. That's why the majority of legal
businesses still persist in operating from wood-lined shrines to
times past. But fustiness doesn't have to be part of the picture when
putting together an office that communicates competence and reli-
ability. Just as heritage fabrics and tailoring have their place in the
wardrobes of today's dapper dressers, the design world is cherishing
classic materials and craftsmanship, and finding ways to twist and
tweak them to bring something fresh to the table, the lamp and the
swivel chair. Here's how to show you mean business – with style.

### DESK

Italian furniture maker Ceccotti employs some of the best design talent around to work on its annual collections, but still follows its own style – a consistency maintained by the skill and signature techniques of its craftsmen. This new American walnut desk by Mr Christophe Pillet is an instant classic.

*ceccotticollezioni.it*

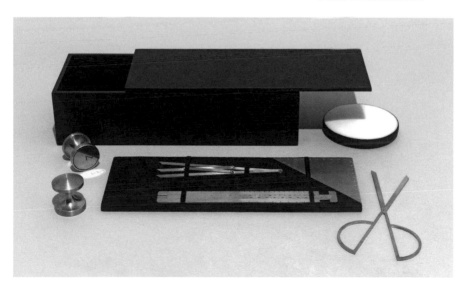

## GEOMETRY SET

Mr Michaël Verheyden began his design career in fashion, but a love of fine materials has stretched beyond leather to marble, precious woods and metals which he mixes to great effect in his home collections. *Wallpaper** commissioned him to design this geometry set in wood, leather and brass for its 2011 Handmade project.

*michaelverheyden.be*

## DESK LIGHT

New Belgian brand Objekten commissions some of Europe's most lauded young designers to produce pared-back household objects. As befits a young company, a lot of energy goes into making products intelligent and ecological – and totally covetable. This swing lamp by Mr Alain Berteau for Objekten has a 270° sweep and can be arranged as a compact sidelight or a desk lamp.

*objekten.com*

### CLOCK

Throw a 20th-century design icon into the mix and see if anyone notices. The City Hall clock was designed in 1956 by the godfather of modern Danish design, Mr Arne Jacobsen, for Rødovre Town Hall. After years in the wilderness it is now once again manufactured in Denmark, by Rosendahl.

*rosendahl-timepieces.com*

### PENS AND PENCILS

We've trusted Moleskine to satisfy our jotter and diary needs and assert a certain authority over our note taking. Now it's time to let its writing instruments do the talking with this creation by designer Mr Giulio Iacchetti, the rectangular carpenter's pencil, meaning they clip neatly against a notebook.

*moleskine.com*

## CHAIR

Creating a chair that will cradle us for most of our waking hours – that supports where necessary and allows us to spin and glide at will while not looking like something from a medical supply shop – is a challenge. Mr Jean-Marie Massaud has done a fine job with his 2006 Aston office chair.

*arper.com*

## WATER CARAFE

Daytime rehydration doesn't have to involve an ever-growing collection of plastic cups from the water cooler. A natty carafe and glasses, such as these by Mr Tomas Kral for PCM – handblown in Spain using 18th-century techniques – will not only up the style stakes, but potentially up your water intake, too.

*pcmdesign.es*

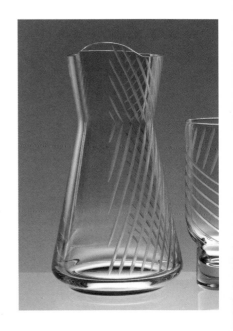

# SWEATSHIRTS

*From athletes to actors, by way of rock stars and writers,
we track the evolution of this style staple*

THE SWEATSHIRT is a casual wardrobe staple, but don't just take
our word for it. Almost every designer has produced a version of this
cotton knit.

Mr Paul Newman, seen here in 1970 on the set of *Sometimes a Great
Notion*, epitomises the sweatshirt's easy-going appeal

The sweatshirt was invented in the early 20th century for athletes. Russell Athletic of Alabama in the US is often credited with its creation. In 1926 the firm's owner developed a cotton sweater for his son to wear for football practice, which was lightweight, easy to move in and less itchy than the woollen jerseys that the team wore. The new garment took off, and sweatshirts came to be worn by athletes while they warmed up, and before or after competition. The smooth surface meant they could be printed with team emblems, as they still are to this day.

The writer Mr Jack Kerouac (*right*; pictured with friend and collaborator Mr Neal Cassady in 1952 ) wears a worn-in sweatshirt just the right way

The reinforced "V" underneath the round collars of most sweat-shirts was traditionally there to absorb sweat; now it is a throwback to when they were mostly worn by sportsmen. Now that sweatshirts are just as popular with the less athletically inclined, the "V" is largely decorative – often simply created using stitching – although if a V-shaped insert of webbing is in place, it can help keep the collar in shape, just as the ribbing on the cuffs and waistband of many sweatshirts maintains a close fit, even after repeated wearing.

Seen here performing with Nirvana in Amsterdam in 1991,
Mr Kurt Cobain underscores the sweatshirt's
rock star appeal

Thanks to their hardwearing nature – and the ease of movement they afford because of their raglan sleeves – sweatshirts soon became popular with mechanics and labourers as well as sportsmen, and have made the transition into workwear – a style that draws on the heritage of what US workers used to wear. However, it is the sweatshirt's inclusion in the preppy, collegiate look that has done most for its style credentials. As Ivy League students started to wear their sports team sweatshirts with chinos and button-down shirts, they became a key part of the Ivy look.

Sweatshirts can be worn in a number of different ways. Staying true to their athletic roots, consider teaming one with shorts and high-top sneakers for an edgy urban look. For something smarter, slip one over a casual shirt, worn with tailored trousers or chinos and a blazer. A sweatshirt in place of a knitted sweater makes an outfit look sportier and less formal, creating an interesting contrast against more structured tailoring. Naturally, sweatshirts are great paired with jeans. Pick a pale, faded pair and add a pair of Converse for a Mr James Dean-inspired look.

Since the sweatshirt is a simple, unfussy item there are few major pitfalls to avoid when it comes to wearing one well. It is, however, always worth avoiding loose, overly baggy sweatshirts, unless you want to look like a fitness instructor from a 1980s home workout video. And for the same reason, under no circumstances should they be worn tucked into jogging bottoms or any other type of trousers. The key to wearing the humble sweatshirt well is to remember that it is an inherently casual item that needs to be matched with a similarly easy-going attitude.

# ROAD TRACKS

*Mr Gustavo Santaolalla – the man behind the music for*
On the Road – *creates a soundtrack to remember*

"Across the Universe"
### THE BEATLES

"Such fantastic lyrics: 'Jai guru deva om/Nothing's gonna change my world…'"

## "Kowali"
### CYRIL PAHINUI

"I love Hawaiian slack key guitar music and I'm a huge fan of the late Gabby Pahinui and his son Cyril."

## "Babylon Sisters"
### STEELY DAN

"A truly evocative song from the 1970s American rock band. It feels free and fun. Perfect for a long drive."

## "Like a Rolling Stone"
### BOB DYLAN

"Bob is a legend and this is a classic. The lyric 'No direction home' encapsulates losing yourself in a trip."

## "To Ohio"
### THE LOW ANTHEM

"A lovely, nostalgic ode to Ohio, but the lyrics can apply to any other place in the world. Simply tailor to your personal destination."

## "Yip Roc Heresy"
### SLIM GAILLARD

"Neal Cassady and Jack Kerouac loved Slim Gaillard and so do I. This has more poignancy with the work I've just completed."

## "Little Floater"
### N R B Q

"'I'm in love with an automobile and I know it's in love with me.' This is a fast-paced, upbeat track, undeniably apt for driving."

## "Space Walk"
### L E M O N  J E L L Y

"Sampling astronaut dialogue, and with a floaty, expansive sound, this song takes you to another place."

## "Lift Me Up"
### J E F F  L Y N N E

"This song has that exact effect, and we all know how much we need a lift sometimes. We must get on with life."

## "Los Ejes De Mi Carreta"
### A T A H U A L P A  Y U P A N Q U I

"Stunning classical guitar work makes this a favourite. There is a morose element to the vocals which provides a reflective effect."

# MR DAMIAN LEWIS

*Meet the star of the hit show that's had us all
– including President Obama – sitting
on the edge of our seats*

MR DAMIAN LEWIS needs no convincing that *Homeland* is a huge hit, perhaps even a career high. Not because of the critical praise or the awards, or even his Best Actor nomination at the Golden Globes. But because in March 2012, he was invited to dinner at the White House, along with Mr George Clooney and main guest Prime Minister David Cameron.

"I thought we were going to be sitting by the kitchen or something," he says. "Next to the revolving door that would repeatedly hit us on the back of the head as waiters came in and out," he continues, slapping the back of his head to demonstrate. "But when we got to the marquee on the South Lawn we found that out of 396 people at this dinner, we had been put at the President's table. I was opposite Obama. He said *Homeland* is his favourite show."

Mr Lewis plays the troubled marine Sergeant Brody, who returns home from Iraq a national hero after years of torture as a prisoner of war. It's the kind of intricate, high-stakes drama that raises the bar on what's possible on television – the first show to capture America's conflicted feelings about the war on terror.

"I knew we were doing something a bit better than your average TV show, or movie for that matter," he says. "But there was no telling the way in which it touched a chord. People get a strange thrill out of being made to feel anxious and worried!"

We meet in Los Angeles, under a bridge downtown, like in the Red Hot Chili Peppers song. Only in this case, we're on a cosy tour bus eating chips and salsa, with a couple of Newcastle Brown Ales on the go.

"Well, you've got to don't you," he says, looking at his wrist. "It's beer o'clock!"

And to be fair, the drink is well earned. Mr Lewis has spent the day getting his picture taken in various outfits all over town, and it's the first day of the May Day protests in the city so traffic has been murder. But he's in good spirits. Life is sweet these days, as he tells me more than once. And besides, he likes a spot of fashion.

"I like that 1960s *Mad Men* thing that's going on," he says. "Equally I can get a bit Burt Reynolds if I wear the right shirt – a few too many buttons undone. It's not a good look, but I just can't avoid it happening!"

He's only in town for a week – a flying visit. Home is Islington, London, with his wife, the actress Ms Helen McCrory, and their two young children, Manon and Gulliver. They live in Mr Hugh Laurie's old house, in fact, another Englishman who's doing rather well on American television.

"Yes, that's how it works. You've got to be English on a popular show and then you get to sell each other property," he grins. "There's an app."

Mr Lewis is more than familiar with Los Angeles at this point in his career. He was introduced to the city by Mr Tom Hanks, of all people. He was cast as the lead in *Band of Brothers* in 2001, a 10-part miniseries that Mr Hanks produced, about a real-life army division in WWII. It was the biggest break of his career by far. How did he get the part?

"That's what President Obama asked me! He thought it was because I looked like the guy I was playing. So I made a joke – I said, 'No Mr President, it was because of my outstanding leadership qualities and moral probity'. And he wasn't sure for a minute – he was like, 'Who the f*** is this guy?'."

In truth, it was classic good fortune – "a needle in the haystack piece of casting", he says. "I'm very lucky." And it established a theme in his career. Mr Lewis has always done well with military roles. He looks the part with his short red hair and chiselled features. He even speaks with a sergeant major's forthright and declarative style.

"It's not as if I come from a military family or anything," he says. "My dad did national service in the 1950s, but he wasn't very good at it. He lost his platoon in the woods."

Mr Lewis grew up on London's Abbey Road, just down from the iconic zebra crossing. And his upbringing was traditional, in the upper middle-class sense. His parents sent him off to boarding schools from the age of eight, including Eton. "If you split everyone up into 'posh' and 'not posh', I'd end up in the posh lot," he says. "But in some ways I've rejected it by choosing to do what I do."

Rather than go to university, he went to Guildhall School of Music and Drama in London, where he rubbed shoulders with the likes of Messrs Ewan McGregor, Daniel Craig and Joseph Fiennes. He wanted to be "an important theatre actor" at first, and duly earned his chops with the Royal Shakespeare Company and the National Theatre. But that didn't last. "It became clear that friends of mine were doing well in the world of high-end TV and movies," he says. "The curiosity just overwhelmed me."

He has never looked back. After *Band of Brothers*, the offers poured in. And top of the list was the lead in a Mr Stephen King movie with Mr Morgan Freeman, an $80m blockbuster. But it tanked horribly, not least because it involved aliens exploding out of people's backsides.

"That was why I took the movie!" he laughs. "All you need for *Dreamcatcher* is a big spliff, a nice comfy sofa and a bag of popcorn."

At the time, it was a bit of a career blow. "I was a young 30, very much on my own and a long way from home. We shot in Vancouver for five months, and I mostly just sat in my hotel room on rainy days not knowing anyone. I think it scared me off a bit."

Better movie experiences would follow – *Keane* in 2004, in which he played a man who loses his daughter, and *The Escapist* in 2008, both did well. And he still takes the occasional movie role – in 2012, he featured in *The Sweeney*, while 2013 sees him in *Romeo & Juliet*.

But television is where Mr Lewis has shone, and on both sides of the Atlantic. In the UK, there was the 2002 remake of *The Forsyte Saga*. And a few years later he was offered the lead in *Life*, a big NBC show back in Los Angeles. It was a period of flux all round. He'd just had a baby and bought his house in Islington, and he wasn't sure what to do. So he called Mr Laurie.

"I'd never met him, I just asked his advice because he was doing so well in LA with *House*. And he said, 'It's lovely working out here, you should take the job and good luck'." He laughs. "He was lying through his teeth!"

*Life* turned out to be a hard slog. For two years he worked 70-hour weeks, often finishing at 4am. And it was harder for his wife, with a second baby arriving in a foreign city, albeit a sunny one.

*Homeland*, however, is a different story – season two was shot in Charlotte, North Carolina on the east side, which doubled as a location for Washington DC.

"It was closer to home. And I didn't have to work so hard because it's more of an ensemble cast. So I just jumped on a plane if I got a few days off. And the kids could come out and see me for the summer holidays, jumping in and out of the pool all day."

He polishes off his beer. "It was perfect, basically. All I had to do was get the acting right – make sure I'm not the tosser who lets it all down!"

# PERFECT TIMING

*Hot from 2012's international watch fairs,*
*MR PORTER chose 10 of the year's finest*

FOR MANY MEN the watch that peeks out from beneath their shirt cuff is what defines their style. Whether it's stainless steel or rose gold, Swiss or Japanese, sporty or elegant, the timepiece a guy chooses to wear says a lot about him, not the least of which is his income bracket. That's why, despite the ubiquity of the time-telling mobile phone, global sales of luxury timepieces have never been stronger. It's against this backdrop that the watch industry, in the form of manufacturers, retailers, journalists and enthusiasts, gathers twice each year in Switzerland – first in January at the Salon de la International Haute Horlogerie (SIHH) in Geneva, and then in spring at Baselworld in Basel – to see what the top brands will be selling through the rest of the year. Here, we take a look at 10 of the best watches from 2012.

I

JAEGER-LECOULTRE
Deep Sea Vintage Chronograph

Inspired by a dive watch originally released in 1959, the new Deep Sea Vintage Chronograph borrows its dial colours and bezel design from its forefather. Under the hood, however, there is a modern chronograph movement that ensures that while it may look 50 years old, the Deep Sea Chronograph runs as true as anything made today. It doesn't hurt that Mr Jean Dujardin, star of *The Artist*, was wearing a Memovox Tribute to Deep Sea when he picked up the Oscar for Best Actor.

*jaeger-lecoultre.com*

1                                                                                                   2

2
AUDEMARS PIGUET
Selfwinding Royal Oak 41mm

In 1972, Audemars Piguet shocked the watch industry when it unveiled the Royal Oak, designed by Mr Gérald Genta. It was the world's first luxury sports watch in stainless steel and broke all the rules of geometry, design, materials and pricing. This audacious piece soon became the watch *de rigueur* of the global jet set and is now a horological icon. In 2012 the entry level selfwinding Royal Oak comes in a new 41mm case size, and is powered by an Audemars-made movement.

*audemarspiguet.com*

3

### 3
### OMEGA
### Speedmaster Racing

While Omega's manually wound Speedmaster Professional gets a lot of attention from watch fans (which it richly deserves, on the grounds that it went to the moon and back), the automatic Speedmasters have always offered a pragmatic alternative. This sporty, colourful chronometer reinforces the brand's connection with motor racing. For the money, you are getting a full package that includes a co-axial escapement.

*omegawatches.com*

### 4
### CARTIER
### Louis Cartier XL Slimline

When the watch moved from the pocket to the wrist, it was thanks to Cartier's Tank. The first commercially successful wristwatch, it has been worn by everyone from General Pershing, back in 1918, to Mr Clark Gable and Mr Muhammad Ali. Cartier emphasises

its classic 1930s aesthetic with this Louis Cartier watch (first introduced in 1922 in this particular case design) with an ultra-slim, mechanical movement. Only Jaeger-LeCoultre's Reverso can rival this watch in the elegance stakes.

*cartier.co.uk*

## 5
### ROLEX
### Sky-Dweller

It's not every year that Rolex releases an entirely new model, and it almost never does so with a complicated watch. In fact, the company hasn't made a really complicated wristwatch since the 1960s. However, at Baselworld 2012, it revealed an entirely new line of watches that couples a GMT function – capable of tracking a second timezone – with an annual calendar, an advanced system that accounts for the varying lengths of each month. The 42mm-sized watch comes in white, yellow and Everose gold.

*rolex.com*

# 6

## TAG HEUER
### Carrera Calibre 17

Mr Jack Heuer is the patriarch of his eponymous brand, and it was he who designed many of the most famous chronographs of the 20th century. TAG Heuer once again handed him the design reins in 2012, in honour of his 80th birthday. The limited edition 41mm Carrera, which is strongly influenced by the original 1960s Carreras, is a classic Heuer (that is what it was called before TAG bought the company in the 1980s) and is branded as such on its dial, and powered by an in-house movement.

*tagheuer.com*

6

7

# 7

## PATEK PHILIPPE
### Nautilus With A White Dial

Nothing is new about this watch except for the colour of the dial, but in the land of Patek Philippe, it's enough to make headlines. The

40mm Nautilus is the quintessential luxury sports watch and while it has, for years, been available with a staid blueish-grey dial, in 2012 it was introduced in an arctic white. The new colour completely changes the tone of this watch and gives it a more youthful look. The Nautilus has a waiting list, so if you're interested in the new 5711 we'd suggest you call your local Patek dealer.

*patek.com*

8

## 8
### BULGARI
### Daniel Roth Papillon Voyageur

A piece for true horological die-hards, the Papillon Voyageur from Bulgari shows two timezones via a bevy of different display mechanisms. The local hour is shown on a large aperture sitting at 12 o'clock, while the GMT hour is indicated with a blue pointer on the main dial. The minutes are then displayed via a semi-circular display and two rotating blue hands that work in conjunction with one another. Sounds complicated? It is, and that's what will attract the 99 guys who are able to buy this limited-edition watch.

*bulgari.com*

## PANERAI
### PAM 438 "Tuttonero"

One of Panerai's strongest suits is its use of interesting materials. In 2011, the Italian-designed but Swiss-made brand delivered one of the highlights of SIHH with a bronze-cased watch, and in 2012, the PAM 438 is not only housed in a ceramic case, but the entire bracelet is ceramic too. The 44mm watch is all but completely scratch proof, and even the in-house automatic movement got the black treatment. Despite the size, this watch is sleek – just imagine how good it would look with a dinner jacket.

*panerai.com*

9      10

## 10
### HARRY WINSTON
### Opus 12

At each Baselworld, the question on everyone's lips is, "Did you see the Opus?" Harry Winston has established itself as a kingmaker of sorts among independent watchmakers, because each year it unveils an Opus model designed by an up-and-coming watchmaker. In 2012 the concept was by Mr Emmanuel Bouchet: time is no longer read by a pair of hands rotating around the central axis but instead by 12 pairs of hands from the outside in. Only a handful will be made, and most are destined for the high-end collectors.

*harrywinston.com*

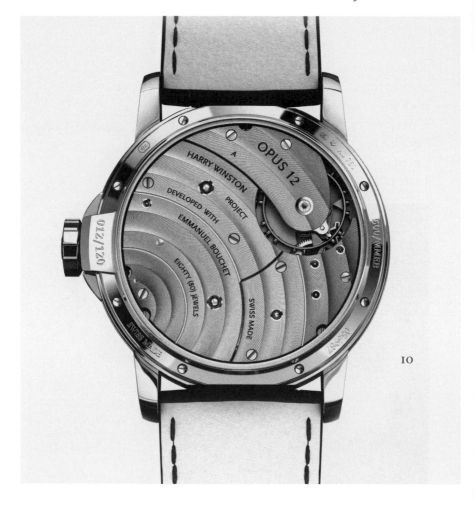

10

# TAKE ME OUT

*Dressing up for a weekend night on the town
is a rite of passage, says Mr Alex Bilmes*

WHERE I'M FROM, in the UK – as, no doubt, it is in many places
around the world – the idea of dressing up for a Friday night out
is mostly a working-class notion, a boy-done-good thing. Blue collar,
if you prefer, although actually the collar would more likely be white,
because in a reverse of the professional-class custom of changing
out of one's business uniform into something more casual to celebrate the coming of the weekend, the working-class dandy comes

home from work, scrapes the grime from beneath his nails and puts on his smartest clothes for a night on the town, the sauce and the dance floor.

This ritual is as deeply ingrained as the dark lines in a labourer's hands. One thinks of Mr Albert Finney as the Nottinghamshire factory worker in *Saturday Night and Sunday Morning*, straightening his tie for an evening of competitive pint sinking. Or Mr John Travolta as the Brooklyn shop worker Tony Manero, slipping into his white three-piece for a night throwing shapes at 2001 Odyssey.

You'll be surprised to learn that I've never done any heavy lifting, but I have always been seduced by the idea of the weekend as a release from the conformist grind of the nine-to-five, an opportunity for ordinary people to become fabulous creatures of the night; a brief respite from the quotidian, with clothes as the most powerful symbols of that temporary escape.

But dressing up to go out changes as you get older. As the 1980s became the 1990s and my teens turned into my twenties I was a committed hedonist, habitué of dubious London night *boîtes* where we danced from Friday nights until Sunday lunchtimes (then we got the beers in). I had a different outfit – a different persona, almost – every weekend. There was the post-punk revivalist: Michiko Koshino bondage trousers, Bikkembergs bovver boots, deconstructed Demeulemeester shirt; the glam rock hanger-on: sparkly Burro shirt, leather John Richmond strides, snakeskin Patrick Cox Wannabes; the New York club kid manqué: Westwood jacket, W&LT T-shirt, Junior Gaultier trousers, eyeliner (don't knock it till you've tried it); the neo-mod likely lad: black Helmut Lang suit, Comme des Garçons grandad collar shirt, identity bracelet. And then there was the stuff I wore when I was feeling a bit more daring.

I realise that other men of my generation may have given no more thought to their Friday night outfit than a splash of Safari and a clean pair of pulling pants, but my youth was about peacockery and flamboyance. When it wasn't Friday night – when it was, say, Tuesday lunchtime – I wore a chocolate brown faux fur coat from Duffer of St. George. It went down a storm on the 36 bus from Peckham to New Cross Gate, let me tell you.

Mr Albert Finney as Arthur and Ms Shirley Anne Field as Doreen
in *Saturday Night and Sunday Morning*, 1960

Times change, fashion moves on, men grow older. In my late twenties and early thirties, at the coalface of 1990s and noughties London medialand, I dressed conservatively: Smedley crew necks and Lacoste polo shirts; Levi's jeans or cargo pants; English brogues or Converse sneakers; Harrington in summer, Barbour in winter. The occasional item from YMC or Margiela 10 if I was feeling flush and flash. The nightclubs were now gastro-pubs. The party pills were razor clams. The dancing was drinking. And I wore the same thing for a Friday night as I did for a Monday morning: too old for skinny jeans, too young for tailoring, instead of going about as someone else, I went as myself. Boring, but more honest.

Times have changed again. The other Friday night I went to a 40th birthday dinner party in a swank west London townhouse. I wore a Richard James corduroy jacket over a Polo Ralph Lauren navy gingham shirt; mustard yellow Drake's tie; A.P.C. jeans; Corgi striped socks and chocolate suede monk-strap shoes from the Tricker's Christmas sale.

The lesson for today – and next Friday night – is: when it comes to dressing up for a night out, acting your age is important.

Herewith are a few observations:

### YOUR TWENTIES

You're young, thin, single and ready to mingle. You can get away with anything. That doesn't mean you should, or you will. We'll take the pulling pants as a given, though J.Crew do good boxers, if you're in the market. You're going to need a decent pair of box-fresh sneakers – high tops if you are really trendy – (we like Common Projects and YSL), jeans from Nudie or Jean.Machine, T-shirt from McQ or B Store, and a Raf Simons or A.P.C. bomber jacket. You, my young friend, are a trendsetter – not a fashion follower. Enjoy it while you can.

### YOUR THIRTIES

You are older, perhaps not thinner, you may or may not be single, but you're still just about ready to mingle. It's in our thirties that we start to learn a bit more about quality, provenance and timeless style rather than disposable fashion. The look is contemporary classicism: Oliver Spencer shirt, battered Grenson brogues, slim-fit cotton-twill trousers from Burberry Brit, Acne jacket. Hip and relevant, but not enslaved to trends.

## YOUR FORTIES

You are as old as you feel. (You're old.) You should know by now that taking off your tie is not enough to separate corporate-guy you from party-guy you. At the same time, the scruffy T-shirt and jeans combo no longer looks dignified. It looks tragic. The look should be relaxed, elegant but still switched on: Richard James blazer or Burberry Prorsum shawl-collar cardigan over Incotex chinos, Margaret Howell shirt. You might even consider a tie: try Alexander Olch. Smart-casual is a horrible term – and curiously indefinable – but for once it's not far wrong.

## YOUR FIFTIES AND BEYOND

Well done, you are on your way to achieving style seniority. You are also freed from the diktats of trendiness. You've earned your right to suavity and are happy to pay for true quality. You are what soft tailoring was invented for: Charvet shirt, Loro Piana blazer, tailored trousers from Canali or Ralph Lauren, John Lobb chocolate suede loafers, Turnbull & Asser pocket square. You are the man the rest of us hope to grow up to be. And you can still cut a rug with the best of them when the moment demands.

THE INTERVIEW

# MR DAVID HOCKNEY

*Outspoken, colourful and undeniably stylish,*
*the great British painter speaks*
*to MR PORTER*

THE HAIR IS GREY, rather than bleach-blond, and the jacket is grey too, rather than gold lamé, but the bright red wool tie is the same, as are the round-framed glasses and the infectious grin. While not quite as strikingly dressed as when he picked up his gold medal from the Royal College of Art in 1962 – with mocking gold jacket and locks to match – it's still unmistakably Mr David Hockney, now the UK's best-loved painter.

Would that younger incarnation recognise the 75 year-old version of himself today, I ask. "Yes, basically I was a cheeky schoolboy then and still am. Most of my friends would think that too." A confident, young, gay man – the epitome of swinging 1960s London, despite having just arrived from provincial Bradford – Mr Hockney was even brazen enough at that time to print up his own mock degree certificate after the RCA threatened to fail him for non-attendance. "It was absurd because they were worried about what diploma to give me, but I told them they should be worried about what they were teaching." The school backtracked and lauded him as its most prized student as soon as it became clear that Mr Hockney would also be the most talked-about artist of his generation.

His decision to quit England for America in 1966 came as something of a shock: "David Hockney, Britain's brightest young artist, has decided to leave Britain", ran the headline in *The Sunday Times*;

"Pop artist pops off" was another. "The first time I went to New York was in 1961," recalls Mr Hockney, "and I must confess the moment I got there I thought, 'This is the place.' It was a more open, 24-hour city. I thought it was fantastic – that is, until I went to Los Angeles."

Seeking sun, sex and freedom, Mr Hockney soon developed a signature West Coast aesthetic through his portrayals of seedy LA street life and the famed pictures of swimming pools and showering boys. "When I went to LA, people told me I'd come to a cultural desert, but I didn't think so. Frankly, when someone tells me that Andy Warhol was the greatest visual artist of the 20th century in America, I say no, I think there's another much bigger – Walt Disney."

In 1997, some 30 years after he first settled in sun-filled Malibu, Mr Hockney returned to his East Yorkshire roots to begin painting its winding lanes and ever-changing seasons – subjects which formed the spine of *A Bigger Picture* – his major show at the Royal Academy of Arts. "I'd always spend Christmases in Bridlington – me, my mother and my sister Margaret – as an only, unmarried son, you can't get out of it. I'd thought it was too dark, I mean you only have six hours of daylight in the winter." Nevertheless, he fell in love with the landscape that was familiar to him from childhood. "The great thing was finding a subject in a rather remote place, where I was left alone. In fact, we can live rather freely in Yorkshire because the office is in LA and they don't get there till six in the evening. Everything happens either in Bridlington or in Hollywood, so we now call it Bridlywood or Hollington."

Indeed, there is something approaching the bravura of cinematic production values in Mr Hockney's most recent forays into the fields and forests of the Yorkshire Wolds. Over the past decade he has produced his largest single works – giant, enveloping multi-partite canvas murals, measuring 40ft wide – as well as experiments with evermore sophisticated technologies, including a new nine-screen film. "Rather than standing still somewhere and looking at something, I started to take in the landscape as a driver quite a long time ago in Southern California, because of its bigger scale. And I did that in Yorkshire, too."

Mr Hockney has never seen things from one static, accepted position, preferring the multiple, non-linear perspective favoured by traditional Chinese artists who, he says, "looked at the world as a walk-through landscape, not through a hole or a window, like Europeans do, which is also the [view of] television or the camera". In the past, Mr Hockney has been a vociferous opponent of the oppressive nature of lens-based media: "To the Chinese, painting was always about the hand, the eye and the heart. Nothing could ever replace it. I mean, how are we going to depict the world, just with photography? It would be rather dull and very restrictive if you know about cameras."

And yet here he is, the 21st-century pin-up boy for the iPad, a device he's been using obsessively since it was released in 2010. So much so, in fact, that when his exhibition opened at the Royal Academy, the main room contained 51 giant iPad prints – nearly one a week for the past year that Mr Hockney had spent drawing the same spot on Woldgate, a road on the outskirts of Bridlington, Yorkshire. "I was painting as fast as possible, the way Van Gogh did," he says. How does he justify his sudden switch from paint to pixels? "There's no such thing as a worn-out subject, it's only the method of depicting the landscape that's worn-out – you find other methods. Every generation can do that. The moment chemical photography ended, we entered a new era of digital photography and Photoshop, which is really drawing. So, in a way the hand is being put back in the camera after the chemicals took it out in 1839."

The other pocket gizmo that has replaced Mr Hockney's usual pens and sketchbooks, the iPhone, goes off loudly and the increasingly deaf artist breaks off from our interview to discuss his health and the stresses of putting on this enormous show, with some physician or other of his, on the other end of the line: "When it's over I'm going to Baden-Baden for a spa." There's still something of the Los Angeleno in him, I suggest. "I haven't left LA. I point that out to my office using the Hollywood phrase, 'I'm on location'."

# THE SHAWL-COLLAR CARDIGAN

*Why this knitwear style is a sure-fire hit*

Mr Steve McQueen on the set of *The Cincinnati Kid*, 1965

DESPITE THE MILITARY CAREER of the Seventh Earl of Cardigan, Lieutenant General James Brudenell, it is his sartorial legacy – the cardigan – that lives on from the 19th century and has seen his title become part of everyday parlance. Legend has it that the Earl invented the style because he wanted a sweater he could put on without tousling his coiffed hair. A more charitable explanation is that the jacket-style knit became popular after the Lieutenant General and his officers wore a similar garment during the Crimean War. Either way, the cardigan has since become a wardrobe staple, and for that we thank the Earl – as well as Ms Coco Chanel and the Ivy League look – for playing a formative part in its history.

The exact point at which the cardigan met the shawl collar, originally found on Victorian smoking jackets, is unclear, although early examples of this hybrid style date from the 1920s. Since the smoking jacket was originally intended to be worn in the home only, and the cardigan is largely concerned with comfort, it seems a natural marriage of elements. Furthermore, the smoking jacket association means that shawl-collar cardigans have a certain louche air about them, banishing the fusty image once associated with button-up knitwear.

The shawl-collar cardigan's unique blend of rakish style and comfort (not to mention the fact that the elongated collar frames the face in a flattering way) has won it legions of fans over the years: from Starsky and Hutch to Mr Daniel Craig, by way of Mr Steve McQueen and Mr Paul Newman, the shawl-collar cardigan has become a style icon in its own right.

Mr Alain Delon on the set of *Les Aventuriers*, 1967

Mr Daniel Craig, London, 2012

# PERFUME GENIUS

*Mr Mike Hadreas, the critically acclaimed, Seattle-based musician, opens up about his five favourite songs*

### "Oh, Sister"
#### BOB DYLAN

"This is the song I am always trying to write. It rolls out so easily, but is almost scientific in how perfectly each word is placed."

### "Only Skin"
#### JOANNA NEWSOM

"It is around 15 minutes long and can turn a dishwashing experience into a light epic. Alternatively, you can lay flat on your face and weep your way through it. She is a total wizard. Her lyrics written out would be important on their own."

### "Flower"
#### LIZ PHAIR

"I remember putting this on as a pre-teen and sitting on my water bed in shock. I lived in constant fear of my sexuality and to hear a woman lay hers down with no apology was truly scary and inspirational."

### "For Your Precious Love"
#### OTIS REDDING

"How can I even say anything? I feel disrespectful attempting to do so. He is telling the truth, you just listen and nod your head."

### "Pacer"
#### THE AMPS

"From the album of the same name, this is one of the few CDs I had in my first apartment in the city. I still feel kind of drunk when I listen to it."

# THE LOOK

# MR HIDETOSHI NAKATA

*Japan's biggest football star talks style, sake
and that all-too-early retirement*

EVERYBODY SAID HE was too young to retire. Mr Hidetoshi Nakata was just 29 when he announced he would be calling it quits, bringing to a close a football career that saw him represent his country in three World Cups and play in the Italian Serie A and English Premier League. But the most famous Japanese footballer of his generation – OK, make that *any* generation – already had other plans: he wanted to travel. "The football world seems very big, but actually it's not," he says. "Every day of my life I played football, so I [only] knew about football... Of course, we travelled a lot for the matches, but we were always in the hotel, stadium, hotel, stadium: we never got to see the cities." Mr Nakata would spend the first few years of his retirement plugging the gaps in his knowledge of the world; today, he estimates that he has visited around 100 countries. And in every one of them, he's found someone who recognised him. "Not because of me," he says, "but because of football."

Well, not *just* football. Mr Nakata wasn't the first Japanese player to try his luck overseas when he signed to Italy's AC Perugia after the 1998 World Cup, but he was the first to become a household name. His impressive displays in Serie A helped, but so did the modelling contracts and a sense of style that drew comparisons to his European counterparts Mr David Beckham and Mr Fredrik Ljungberg. (In 2010, he even followed Mr Ljungberg's example to become a Calvin Klein Underwear model.)

Mr Nakata says it was during a month-long training session in Italy when he was 18 years old that his sense of style really began to develop. "Obviously, if you go to Italy, you go for football, but fashion is all around you," he says. Before long, he was spending his pay packets on expensive outfits and dying his hair a range of different colours.

There was a considerable media hubbub at home when he gave himself a peroxide rinse in advance of the 1998 World Cup, in what was thought to be an attempt to get noticed by European scouts (if so, it worked a charm). But these days, Mr Nakata is not inclined to be so ostentatious. "Before, fashion was something to look at: I wanted to be fashionable," he continues. "Now it's like a part of my life, so I don't need to really think about it. Every day, I'll take a shower and then eat – [it's on] the same level."

His tastes have evolved, too, extending from fashion to architecture, interior design and craftsmanship – "because that influences you a lot in your life". All these experiences have come in handy for his latest mission. After travelling around the world, Mr Nakata is now rediscovering his native country. He's spent the past few years scouring each of Japan's 47 prefectures for their best arts, crafts, shrines, temples and *ryokan* (inns), starting in the far-flung southern islands of Okinawa and steadily working his way north. When we meet, he only has eight prefectures left to visit.

It was in the course of these travels that he picked up his latest obsession: sake. Japan's traditional rice wine is a drink with a rich history and an image problem – a tipple that could do with some high-profile help as sales decrease in Japan. And after visiting 150 of Japan's top breweries, Mr Nakata will be launching his own brand, sold exclusively overseas – where consumption is on the rise – and aimed at high-end restaurants.

"Before, I thought maybe it would be nice to have my own vinery or wine brand," he says. "But after visiting sake makers, I said: 'I'm Japanese, so maybe I should have my own sake label'.

"At the same time, it would be cool to have one of the best sakes in the world. It's like having a Château Mouton Rothschild or Gaja – if you are the owner of that kind of wine. You go to good restaurants in London, in New York, and then you can order your own sake. That's cool."

# THE BOMBER JACKET

*Why the jacket of choice for presidents, heroes and
rebels alike is the essence of enduring style*

ENDLESSLY VERSATILE, and rather flattering thanks to its shape,
the humble bomber can be dressed up with a preppy shirt and tie
just as easily as it can be thrown on with jeans and sneakers.

Epitomising the vintage aviator look, with flying goggles to boot,
Mr Gregory Peck is pictured here on the set of the 1949 war movie
*Twelve O'Clock High*

Back when aircraft cockpits were unheated and open to the elements, pilots required specialised jackets that would keep them warm without restricting movement. The resulting design, which was first developed by the US Army Aviation Clothing Board in 1917, marks the origins of the bomber jacket. Four years later, Lieutenant John Macready set an altitude record while wearing one, flying in an open-cockpit plane to 40,000 ft. Early versions were constructed from leather or shearling, with the transition towards lighter materials occurring as aerospace technology advanced: cockpits became enclosed, heated and even less spacious (due to an increased amount of equipment and more streamlined airframes), necessitating the need for less bulky jackets. The bomber's design characteristics have, however, remained largely unchanged: the

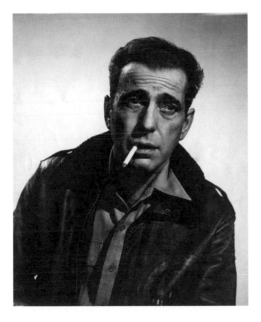

Mr Humphrey Bogart, pictured on the set of *Tokyo Joe*, 1949, demonstrates that attitude can be just as important as clothes when it comes to style

cropped length (they were designed to be worn sitting down), the roomy sleeves and unstructured shoulders for ease of movement, the snug cuffs and waistbands, and numerous pockets (including the easy-access pen pocket on the sleeve) remain hallmarks of most bombers today.

Before the practice was prohibited, it was common for Air Force crews to customise their jackets with squadron patches, rank marks and regimental emblems. Elaborate designs were often painted on the backs of the jackets depicting the type of aircraft flown, the artwork painted on the jet itself (pin-up girls were commonly featured), the number of successful missions completed or targets hit.

Some airmen would sew maps into the lining of their jackets in case they were shot down in unfamiliar territory, while others would attach "blood chits" – notices printed in foreign languages promising civilians rewards for assisting the pilot if he was downed. Different coloured linings were sometimes used to signify war-related achievements: for example, in some units, a red satin lining would be given to an airman who had completed his fifth aerial kill.

Customised or not, the bomber jacket has long been a favourite item among troops, to the extent that the US military has occasionally been forced to limit production to keep costs down, despite unwavering demand. This makes its transition into the civilian wardrobe, and popular culture, unsurprising.

From US presidents, who sport shearling-collared flight jackets when they wish to affirm their commander-in-chief credentials, to 1990s hip-hop stars by way of the skinheads in *This is England*, and also Ivy Leaguers, whose varsity jackets are an approximation of the style, the bomber is a versatile, modish jacket with timeless appeal. And if any further proof is needed, the most talked about men's style on the screen last year was Mr Ryan Gosling's bomber jacket in *Drive*.

Along with jeans, the bomber jacket was thrust into the fashion
mainstream by Mr James Dean's appearance in the 1955 movie
*Rebel Without a Cause*

# MR IRVINE WELSH

*When* Skagboys, *his* Trainspotting *prequel came out,*
*the controversial author talked bad behaviour,*
*1970s punk and clean-cut shirts*

UNCHARACTERISTICALLY of a Scotsman, Mr Irvine Welsh orders a green tea from the waiter as we sit in London's Ivy Club, explaining that he's feeling somewhat fragile after a protracted two-city celebratory whirl to toast his latest novel *Skagboys*. First it was a night in Dublin with his pals, then a champagne supernova of a party with publishers and publicists over in London... followed by a self-prescribed detoxification.

Hangover clearing now, Mr Welsh is allowing himself to quietly gloat over the surprise success of what is essentially a "*Trainspotting* prequel". "The book business has been all about genre fiction for so long, so it's rare that a book such as this can sell so many copies," says Mr Welsh.

*Do you think part of your success has been writing books that are read by people who don't normally read novels?*
I think that was probably true when I first started. Certainly, *Trainspotting* fell into that category. You had this new bunch of kids coming through who told me that it was the first book they ever picked up. Now, two decades later, I have this crusty but loyal generation who have grown up with me and stuck with me and now tend to be a generally really rather well-read bunch. That said, the

success of this book [*Skagboys*] has definitely been helped by what I call the "*Trainspotting* effect". Revisiting those old characters has sparked a lot of interest, but people who have read my work will know it's actually something I've always done with my books; characters familiar from previous stories will gate-crash their way into parts of all my novels from time to time.

*You've lived in London, Amsterdam, Dublin, Leith and Edinburgh. Where do you live now? And why do you keep moving?*
I'm based in Chicago now but I also have a place in Miami and because of all the stuff I have going on in Hollywood, I also spend a lot of time in Los Angeles. I've done everything officially this time, got the green card, the lot, so it feels fairly permanent. And a bit scary if I'm honest. For years I've always had this London/Edinburgh axis… but living in America is working for me because I find I have different cities for different parts of my career.

*Miami, Chicago, Dublin… they are all quite Irvine Welsh-ish sorts of places aren't they? Cities with a certain edge, a seedy side to them. Does city life still inspire your writing?*
Oh I think every city has that side to it these days. I love being in Chicago with my musician friends and DJs. I hang out with boxers and go to the racetrack and the baseball, which all sounds like the stuff of novels, doesn't it? But for some reason I don't really feel moved to write about Chicago. It was the same when I was living in Dublin. These places are great but also so ossified and tied down in a way, with everything in its right place. The other thing, of course, is that there are already plenty of writers living in those places so the competition is fierce. Miami is much more interesting to me because it's a city in total flux, and constantly emerging. It has design and art, loads of bars, a thriving downtown area and a new baseball team, but it's also very noir-ish. It's no accident that TV shows such as *Dexter, Miami Vice* and *CSI* are based there and that writers such as

Carl Hiaasen are attracted to the city because Miami has this really captivating mixture of the dark and glossy.

*Tell us about your writing process. Do you have a grand, soundproofed study or do you prefer the kitchen table?*

In Chicago I have this huge room, which I rather pretentiously call my "writing suite". I got the idea after visiting Ernest Hemingway's house in Key West – he had a "writing suite" so I thought I'd have one too. Mine has oak panels on one side, lined with all my books. Opposite, there's a huge TV screen intended to help me with my screenwriting work. I have my DJ decks in one corner and another wall covered in scribbled notes, story arcs, clippings and photos, which is like something out of *CSI*. There's a balcony where I can hang out and watch people heading off to work. But in Miami I just have this grotty little bedroom, which is really no more than a box, and if I'm being honest, I probably do all my best writing there.

*Have you ever worn suits?*

When I was dabbling in the property business back in the early 1990s, I was heavily influenced by Kevin Rowland's clean-cut, *Don't Stand Me Down* period – the Brooks Brothers suits and all that. I was messed up on heroin at the time but I was also keen to appear very businesslike, so rather perversely I decided to look straight on the outside and dressed yuppie-style, mainly in suits. In Miami I used to slob around in shorts and T-shirts but I've now gone completely the other way – I go to this old-school Florida tailor and wear suits in linen and seersucker. Pastel colours, mainly. I have all the accessories: cufflinks, pocket handkerchiefs and a Panama hat, too; the whole Humphrey Bogart/*Key Largo* look. I dress better in Miami than I do in any other city. Even though I get very hot, I would never go out in Miami without a suit on.

*Do you still go clubbing these days, or get to DJ?*
I'll go to Fabric while I'm in London but generally I don't really go
to clubs much any more, because I don't enjoy being the oldest guy
in the room – which I have been for the past 20 years, by the way. If
you go for it too much, you look ridiculous, like the weird uncle at
the wedding. So, what I do instead is I get my decks out and have
parties at my house with some local music people – people of my
own age. And no young people around to laugh at us.

# SUNDAY GIRL

*Sultry songstress Ms Jade Williams*
*chooses her top tracks*

### "Love Me"
STOOSHE

"Stooshe are an insane three-piece girl band, like TLC or something. They feature on the BBC's Sound of 2012 list. Their songs are so naughty and this track is a great example of that."

## "Born to Die"
### LANA DEL REY

"There is loads of controversy around Lana Del Rey – there are lovers and haters – but I think she's brilliant. Everybody wishes they'd come up with the concept for that video. It annoys me when people say she's manufactured; so she may have a bit of collagen in her lips, but she writes all her own songs and she's a true talent."

## "Mama do the Hump"
### RIZZLE KICKS

"I love Rizzle Kicks as they do all their own videos and it comes across very authentically. Their video for this track has James Corden in it doing their dance. Brilliant."

## "Somebody That I Used to Know"
### GOTYE

"This song gets stuck in your head. I find myself singing it at the top of my voice whenever it comes on the radio."

## "Big in Japan"
### MARTIN SOLVEIG

"Martin Solveig is a genius and the nicest man ever! Every song on his new album, *Smash*, is a hit. 'Big in Japan' is so fun."

# MR JOHN PAWSON

*The pioneering architect has an unerring eye for style –*
*with everything he touches*

THE BRITISH ARCHITECT Mr John Pawson is recalling his earliest architectural memories over breakfast in his kitchen in West London's Notting Hill. "As children we used to go to Fountains Abbey and Rievaulx Abbey, Cistercian monastic ruins in Yorkshire. I noticed something – the great thing about architecture is that you respond to it physically, it makes you feel good." The early spring sunshine that's falling through the glass wall that separates the kitchen from the garden underlines the master of modern minimalism's point.

However, it was the friendship he formed in his twenties with Japanese designer Mr Shiro Kuramata that took Mr Pawson from appreciation to action. He explains, "His work was the first physical manifestation of what I had in my head. He was the one who persuaded me to go to architecture school." So after a brief stint studying at London's Architectural Association School of Architecture Mr Pawson went into practice, starting with his then-girlfriend's apartment, swiftly followed by the West End art gallery where she worked. His designs were shocking for their purity and quickly attracted attention – not least that of the famous British author Mr Bruce Chatwin, who wrote an essay about Mr Pawson's apartment.

Reassuringly, the architect has consoling words for men who set more store by their possessions than the nomadic Mr Chatwin: "It's not about asceticism, there's just a pleasure in seemingly empty

spaces. It's difficult not to accumulate stuff and it's a full-time job keeping what you have to a minimum, but there are benefits." Mr Pawson's wish to resist the lure of material possessions is, he says, something that's been with him since childhood. "I've hated having to worry about material things ever since [as a child] I lost some Parker pens on Blackpool beach, that's when I vowed not to be attached to things any longer."

Mr Pawson takes a similarly unsentimental approach to his clothes. "I'm often on building sites," he says. "I like not to have to worry about clothes, not to have to think. I like simple rugged things. Catherine [his wife] is always trying to get me into a blue shirt, but I find that when I look down I prefer to see white." However, after years of only wearing pale grey cable-knit sweaters, his outfits are not entirely unchanging. "Now I'm also wearing brown cashmere sweaters and I'm wearing black jeans, too," he says. Given that his work is defined by the use of beautiful materials, Mr Pawson's "simple rugged things", while unfussy, are hardly basic, as he explains: "I've got a collection of Loro Piana pullovers – a crew-neck pullover is a convenient bit of kit. Paul Smith is a good bet for shirts and I get my socks there – I like long black socks; I don't like to see hairy legs."

For anyone keen to understand Mr Pawson's view of the world he has published an inspiring book, *A Visual Inventory*. It's a collection of beautiful photographs, taken from 250,000 images he's shot over 10 years. "It's my sketchbook, I use the camera to record anything that catches my eye," he explains. "Rather than what I see, it's how I see." One of the things the book reveals is how many wonderful places Mr Pawson gets to visit. From Bavarian barns to Arizona air bases via Ethiopian churches and Swiss modernist villas, the reader is taken on a remarkable architectural tour.

The boot is on the other foot in West London, where he has carved a new home for Britain's Design Museum out of a striking 1960s-era building, which houses the work of other architects and designers. "It's incredible to have a building with that much space in the middle of a park [Holland Park] in central London," he enthuses. "The roof soars 16m above the top floor, so it's an exciting interior space."

The medieval monasteries that originally inspired Mr Pawson gave him an understanding of the way buildings can affect a person, which has informed all his projects, from fashion stores to a modern-day monastery. As he explains, "When it's architecture there's an excitement, an atmosphere, something special. The rest is just building."

THE WORK

BARON HOUSE, SKÅNE, SWEDEN, 2005
The sloping surrounds conceal Mr Pawson's design, whose elements borrow the local vernacular, from the nearby road, yet even when visible its clean white lines appear to recede into the expansive sky

ABBEY OF OUR LADY OF NOVÝ DVŮR, BOHEMIA,
CZECH REPUBLIC, 2004
This sparse monastery, the first built in the country since the Velvet
Revolution, dovetails with the monks' asceticism: "An absence
of visual and functional distraction supports the goal of
monastic life," Mr Pawson says of his work

MARTYRS PAVILION, OXFORD, ENGLAND, 2009
Raised on a mound to maximise views and with its linear marble base
imitating the field's chalk creases, Mr Pawson's design serves as
a public landmark, yet adheres to the functionality of a
classic British cricket pavilion

# POLO SHIRTS

*From sporting origins to silver-screen style,*
*we chart the ageless appeal of this*
*summer essential*

Pictured here off Newport, Rhode Island, in August 1962,
President John F. Kennedy demonstrates the
polo's leisurely appeal

THE TERM "CLASSIC" is thrown about liberally in menswear, but the polo shirt is one item to which it can truly be applied: its design has not changed since it was developed in the early 20th century, and it looks as good today as it did then. It would be quicker to name contemporary designers who have not produced polo shirts than it would be to go through the exhaustive list of those who have. Bridging the formality gap between a shirt and a T-shirt, the polo is an invaluable wardrobe component.

In 1926 the French tennis champion Mr René Lacoste developed what is now known as the polo shirt. Previously, tennis players wore long-sleeved button-up shirts and ties on the court, but Mr Lacoste tired of this restrictive uniform, and instead came up with a short-sleeved, loosely knitted cotton shirt. Its distinctive features, which the polo shirt retains today, were a flat folded-over collar (which could be upturned to keep the sun off the neck), a buttoned placket extending no more than a third of the way down the front of the shirt, a breathable knitted fabric, short-cuffed sleeves and a slightly longer back than the front (to ensure it would not ride up during matches). Mr Lacoste called his invention the tennis shirt and began selling it in 1933.

### THE EVOLUTION

Later in the 20th century, polo players also adopted a variant of Mr Lacoste's tennis shirt in a similar departure from their traditional, restrictive uniform. The reason that the name "polo shirt" has endured rather than "tennis shirt" is in no small part down to Mr Ralph Lauren's decision to make this style of shirt, embroidered with a pony motif, a permanent part of his collection in 1973. Polo shirts have also found favour with golfers – those with a pocket on the front (to store a pencil and scorecard) are sometimes known as golf shirts. Similarly, various style tribes have adopted the polo, from 1960s mods to preppy College boys.

Pictured here in Paris in 1995, the same year his seminal movie
*La Haine* was released, Mr Vincent Cassel updates
the polo with urban attitude

### WHEN TO WEAR A POLO SHIRT

Although it is smarter than a T-shirt, the polo shirt is inherently
casual (its design was born out of comfort and the stripping away
of formality) so it is best not worn for formal occasions. Whenever
you are off duty, though, the polo goes particularly well with jeans,
chinos, shorts, cardigans and casual jackets – including bombers,
safari jackets and single-breasted, unstructured blazers. Wearing a
polo shirt with a highly tailored, formal blazer is a look best avoided,
not least because the collar tends to get lost beneath the blazer's

Seen here arriving in London in 1965, Mr Terence Stamp shows you need nothing more than jeans, boots and a watch to make a polo shirt look great – although the right attitude never goes amiss either

lapels, and wearing the polo shirt's collar on the outside of the jacket is rarely advisable. With the right blazer, though, the polo is acceptable for "smart casual" events.

### TO TUCK OR NOT TO TUCK

There are occasions when a polo shirt can look good tucked into your trousers (provided you have a flat stomach, of course), but we generally favour an untucked look, not least because tucking it in rather goes against the polo's casual, unrestrictive DNA. If you're going to dress a polo shirt up with a softly tailored blazer or suit, it's best to leave it untucked – otherwise you lose the interesting formal/informal contrast and might as well stretch to wearing a regular shirt. A good example of why to be careful with your tucking comes via Mr Tom Hanks in his movie *Larry Crowne*. When the cute and somewhat perversely attentive Talia asks Larry, "Are you an ex-cop?" he replies, "No, why would you think that?" To which she says, "Tucking in your polo shirt makes you look like one." Need we say more.

With the contentious tucking issue out of the way, there are a few other pointers to cover. Avoid free promotional polo shirts and/or those adorned with corporate logos (Paperclip Department 2009 Team Building Day, really?) like the plague. Make sure your polo shirt isn't too long or baggy: it should fall right at the waist, and never hang lower than hip level. Excess fabric, especially around the waist, will make you look heavier than you are. If the collar gets limp after repeated washing, use some spray sizing (a softer version of starch) to restore its crispness. Finally, don't be afraid to experiment with colour; polo shirts look great in bright shades, particularly when the sun is shining and you have a long drink in hand.

# STYLE ICONS
# 32 MEN WHOSE DRESS SENSE WE ADMIRE

### MR JEAN-PAUL BELMONDO

Mr Jean-Paul Belmondo was a leading light in French New Wave cinema and was acclaimed for his roles in Mr Jean-Luc Godard's *Breathless* (1960) and Mr Alain Resnais' 1974 film *Stavisky*. His style is anchored by his exemplary choice of clothes and the palpable sense that he doesn't give a damn. It's a potent combination.

## MR STEVE MCQUEEN

Mr Steve McQueen is a style icon regular. And, to avoid being predictable, we really did try to leave him out of this one. But it just felt wrong. Come on, the guy starred in *The Great Escape*, *Bullitt* and *The Thomas Crown Affair*, loved racing motorbikes, married Ms Ali MacGraw, and wore chinos and Persols like no one else.

### MR BOB DYLAN

There aren't many songwriters whose words have become anthems for civil rights and anti-war movements. One of the most influential cultural figures of the 20th century, we're going to be very superficial and just point out how good a man can look when he finds the right black leather jacket.

MR CRISTÓBAL BALENCIAGA

Mr Cristóbal Balenciaga was the Spanish designer who, in 1937, founded his world-famous eponymous fashion house in Paris. He was responsible for dressing some of the most powerful women of his generation (the Queen of Spain, the Queen of Belgium, the Duchess of Windsor and Princess Grace of Monaco) and regarded as "the master" by many, including Mr Christian Dior and Ms Coco Chanel. A devotee to monochrome tailoring, Mr Balenciaga became synonymous with the sharp double-breasted suit.

## MR GIOVANNI AGNELLI

Mr Giovanni "Gianni" Agnelli was an Italian industrialist, president of Fiat and, according to many at the time, the true king of Italy. While he ruled over the Italian economy and European high society during the 1960s, 1970s and 1980s, he was admired as much for his dress sense as for his business acumen. He mastered the art of *sprezzatura* – making the difficult look easy. His style trademarks included wearing a watch over his shirt sleeve (saves time) and leaving his tie slightly askew, or hanging over his sweater.

## LORD GLENCONNER

Colin Tennant, Third Baron Glenconner, was famous for having fun. And who can criticise a guy for that? He bought the West Indian island of Mustique – most of us make do with just booking a hotel – and transformed it into a multimillionaire's playground in the late 1960s. A gregarious host, and close friend of Princess Margaret, Lord Glenconner dressed like the quintessential tropical patriarch, peppering his wardrobe with bright colours, tunics and wide-brimmed hats. And it somehow worked.

### MR RIVER PHOENIX

The early death of Mr Phoenix, who died aged 23 in October 1993, deprived us of both a great actor and a future style icon. In photographs he emerges as a man of grace and elegance. The image of him in a dinner jacket is a reminder of the spirit in which the tuxedo, the quintessence of male elegance, should be worn.

### MR TAHAR RAHIM

This French actor, from Belfort on the country's eastern border, came to international attention in the 2009 film *The Prophet*, a tense prison drama directed by Mr Jacques Audiard. Although in the 2011 film *The Eagle* he wore an extraordinary camouflage suit made of animal skin we're more interested in Mr Rahim's ability to look both chic and relaxed, in an inimitably Gallic way.

LORD BYRON

It's a testament to Lord Byron's 19th-century romantic poetry that, despite his extraordinary life story, he remains best known for his literary talents. Although described in 1812 by Lady Caroline Lamb as "mad, bad, and dangerous to know" we retain a guilty admiration for his romantic exploits, as well as for the claret shade of his velvet robes.

### MR DAVID BOWIE

Sartorial chameleon Mr David Bowie could easily be five different style icons, but to our eyes his best-dressed era was the late 1970s and early 1980s, when he mined a seam of fashionable tailoring that demonstrates that it's possible to wear the traditional elements of menswear but make them entirely your own. Although few other men could carry off this sage-green suit, many could take a leaf out of his book with regards to the bow tie and plaid shirt combination.

## MR MARCELLO MASTROIANNI

Mr Marcello Mastroianni, the suave Italian actor, became synonymous with style after his role as the playboy journalist in Mr Federico Fellini's *La Dolce Vita*. There was substance to the man, too: he is one of only three actors to win Best Actor twice at Cannes. And he fathered a child with Ms Catherine Deneuve. Respect.

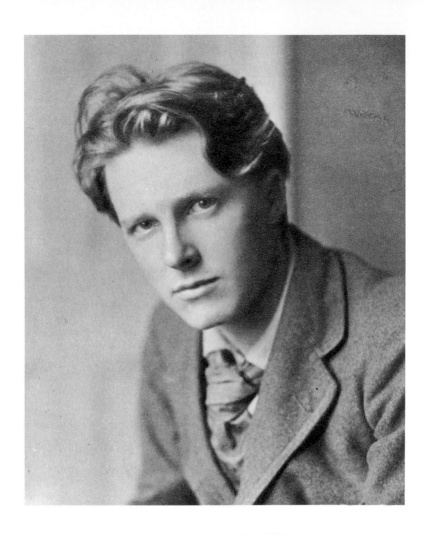

MR RUPERT BROOKE

The English poet behind "The Soldier" ("If I should die, think only this of me/ That there's some corner of a foreign field that is forever England") was a very modern character despite being born in the 19th century. In 1915 he died of a septic mosquito bite on his way to Gallipoli, but he found time before then to embrace a romantic vision of elegance that has a very contemporary appeal.

### MR PAUL NEWMAN

Mr Paul Newman was just so darned good looking, and so impeccably attired, and so absurdly talented, we should all truly hate him. But to add insult to injury, the award-winning star of *Cat on a Hot Tin Roof*, *The Hustler* and *Cool Hand Luke* was also an incredibly good guy. This shot shows that, back in the 1960s, he had the whole preppy look down to a T.

MR EDWARD FOX

The fact that the Duke of Windsor and the Jackal, two of the characters for which this British actor is best known, were beautifully dressed on screen is due in part to Mr Fox's interest in clothes. He remains impeccably turned out in Savile Row suits and handmade shoes, and only lets his sartorial guard down when he pulls on the worn corduroys in which he gardens.

## MR LUDWIG MIES VAN DER ROHE

One of the preeminent modernist architects, Mr Mies van der Rohe was born in Germany, but left for Chicago in 1937. In his architecture he used the finest materials to create some of the 20th century's most beautiful buildings. He was no less exacting in his choice of clothes, as demonstrated by his exquisitely cut suits, at least some of which came from Viennese tailors Knize.

### MR WARIS AHLUWALIA

Born in India, Mr Waris Ahluwalia emigrated to America as a child. Some years later and his jewellery line has gained as much attention as his acting career, the highlights of the latter being roles in two films by Mr Wes Anderson. But it's the ease with which Mr Ahluwalia wears clothes that inspires our admiration, as he demonstrates here with a casual deployment of a blue trench coat.

MR LOUIS GARREL

Mr Louis Garrel comes from a cinematic family of film-makers and actors. He achieved worldwide recognition with Mr Bernardo Bertolucci's 2004 film *The Dreamers* and has been providing a masterclass in louche Gallic style ever since, something reinforced by his relationship with Ms Carla Bruni's older sister Ms Valeria Bruni Tedeschi.

### SIR MICHAEL CAINE

One of the sharpest dressers in 1960s London, Sir Michael Caine eschewed the era's peacock style in favour of the kind of restrained but energetic tailoring that's entirely relevant today. Sir Michael relied on the late tailor Mr Douglas Hayward, but thankfully suits in cuts such as the one above are now more readily available.

## MR CLINT EASTWOOD

When we're feeling lucky we aspire to look this good in a tweed jacket; Mr Clint Eastwood is simultaneously masculine and nonchalant in his semi-formal outfit. He demonstrates that tweed jackets work as outerwear, that there's no substitute for decent cloth and that an attitude is the ultimate accessory.

### MR JEAN-LUC GODARD

Not only was film director Mr Jean-Luc Godard able to create a vision of timeless cool when he made *À bout de souffle* (who wouldn't want to be Mr Jean-Paul Belmondo with Ms Jean Seberg at his side?) but he has exhibited a very modern style throughout his career. No man ever lost his hair with such nonchalance.

## HIS IMPERIAL MAJESTY HAILE SELASSIE

His Imperial Majesty Haile Selassie was the Emperor of Ethiopia
from 1930 to 1974. In fact, his full title was: His Imperial Majesty
Haile Selassie I, King of Kings, Lord of Lords, Conquering Lion
of the Tribe of Judah, and Elect of God. He was also, at the time
of his reign, the most bemedalled ruler in the world. Befitting for
someone who could trace his ancestry back to King Solomon and
the Queen of Sheba, Selassie could rock up a regal look or two.

**MR TRUMAN CAPOTE**

The American author, most famous for writing literary classic *Breakfast at Tiffany's*, was a dandy whose frivolous image belied the gravity of his dedication to his occupation. His personal style was exuberant, and chimes with the kind of prints that are now firmly back in fashion.

MR CLARK GABLE

The star of *Gone With the Wind* is remembered as an impecca-bly groomed smoothie. Few men have worn clothes as well as Mr Gable, whose appearance in his publicity photographs prob-ably explains why the co-stars he enjoyed romantic success with included Ms Grace Kelly and Ms Joan Crawford.

MR GREGORY PECK

The Californian actor Mr Gregory Peck made his first film, *Days of Glory*, in 1944, and by 1949 he'd been Oscar-nominated for four different movies. Among his famous roles he played Atticus Finch in the film version of *To Kill a Mockingbird*, in which he set the bar high for men aspiring to wear off-white, three-piece suits, and Joe Bradley in *Roman Holiday*, in which he was sufficiently stylish to capture the heart of Ms Audrey Hepburn.

### MR TOM WAITS

Mr Tom Waits' voice has been described by rock critic Mr Daniel Durchholz as "like it was soaked in Bourbon, left hanging in the smokehouse for a few months, and then taken outside and run over with a car". And the singer's style is correspondingly rugged, whether he's dressed in a suit or, as here, in classic workwear.

MR RYAN O'NEAL

The star of the 1970 film *Love Story*, in which he appeared alongside the beautiful Ms Ali MacGraw, is a style icon whose look continues to stay on-trend. The traditional collegiate clothes he wore in the film included a taste for corduroy, tweed, sheepskin and chunky Aran sweaters.

### SIR MICK JAGGER

Admittedly, it shouldn't be too hard for a skinny, long-haired rock star to figure out how to work a look. Especially in the 1960s. But this Rolling Stone nailed it immediately. And Sir Mick Jagger has continued to do so ever since. He has shown that colour, pattern and a good fit can work for even the most red-blooded of us.

### MR ROBERT REDFORD

Very cool in its own right, Mr Robert Redford's style really comes alive when he's in character, and never more so than when he was dressed by Mr Ralph Lauren for 1974's *The Great Gatsby*. Between the sumptuous suits and Mr Redford's aristocratic bearing, the film is a masterclass in how to dress up.

MR NEIL "BUNNY" RODGER

Aside from his eye-catching Edwardian style this British dandy was also a WWII combat hero and a dress designer. He ordered 15 suits a year from his Mayfair tailor, and is said to have had four pairs of shoes made for every one. He maintained his slim figure the better to show off his unusual four-button suits.

### THE DUKE OF WINDSOR

Although the list of his other virtues is short the duke is widely
considered to be the best-dressed man of the 20th century and his
clothes were exemplary in many ways. He was best known for the
suits that were superbly tailored for him, primarily by Mr Freder-
ick Scholte on Savile Row.

## MR DAVID BECKHAM

The British football star has grown up in public, and part of that progression has been his developing sense of style. As he moves from the sports field to a more ambassadorial role his look is becoming increasingly formal, and he's frequently seen in slim tailoring that's entirely contemporary and entirely correct. His casual clothes are also becoming more stylish, and this combination is a masterclass in smart weekend wear.

### MR SIDNEY POITIER

In 1963 Mr Poitier became the first black man to win the Oscar for Best Actor, for his performance in *Lilies of the Field*. It came at a time when he was politically active in the civil rights movement, and photographs of the period show him on marches impeccably dressed in a slim black suit, white shirt and black tie. However, he was no less elegant off-duty, as this relaxed outfit demonstrates.

# MR MATTHEW DEAR

*The hip Texan DJ and producer tips us off on his
top five tunes to start the New Year*

### "New Year's Eve"
TOM WAITS

"Since its release Tom Waits' latest album, *Bad As Me*, has been heavily played in my house. As soon as his songs start, you're thrust into the middle of a dense story already in motion. It's as if you've opened a door onto a dimly lit ancient scenario that was going on with or without you being there."

### "Love is Blindness"
U2

"*Achtung Baby* captures a timeless, provocative world. It is by far one of my favourite rock albums of all time. This track echoes some woeful lust-laden love."

### "All the Tired Horses"
BOB DYLAN

"'All the tired horses in the sun. How am I supposed to get any ridin' done?' This lyric, sung by a small group of female vocalists, repeats throughout the song. It is pure and simple, glorious music."

### "Brand New Companion"
#### TOWNES VAN ZANDT

"While I hear there is quite a bit of Townes' unreleased material out there being safely guarded, I still haven't tired of everything you can readily find. His songs are dense, wrapped in poetic layers, and I learn something new with every listen. This track is an inspirational blues number."

### "A Pause for Reflection"
#### TRENT REZNOR & ATTICUS ROSS

"Listening to their soundtracks is like listening to an organism, expanding and contracting with every heaving breath. It's almost as if they have built a sound laboratory, and listening to it is an amazing experience. There is a beautiful process at play here."

# GRIZZLY BEAR

*The founder of the Brooklyn-based band, Mr Ed Droste,
picks five tracks he has on repeat*

### "Motion Sickness"
#### HOT CHIP

"They just keep getting better. I've been a fan of them from the start
and this is a real grower for me."

### "Hit 'Em Wit Da Hee"
#### MISSY ELLIOTT

"I've been revisiting Missy's first album recently in anticipation of something new from her and this cut is one of my favourites from an album of no duds. It hasn't aged a day for me."

### "Myth"
#### BEACH HOUSE

"This band remains one of my favourites. We've had the honour of getting to tour with them a bunch and they just keep on getting better. They even played at my wedding!"

### "Cyan"
#### KINDNESS

"I love the Arthur Russell flavour in this song, but the whole album is super diverse and amazing. Adam Bainbridge can do no wrong if you ask me. Amazing live show to boot."

### "Get Free" (featuring Ms Amber Coffman of Dirty Projectors)
#### MAJOR LAZER

"Damn, I love Amber's voice. Everything she sings grabs hold of me, and this Major Lazer song is so great mostly because she really owns it."

# MR CHARLES SCHUMANN

*The legendary founder of Schumann's bar in Munich
creates a stylish cocktail especially for*
MR PORTER

AS HE PREPARES three of his favourite cocktails for MR PORTER, Mr Charles Schumann proclaims, "I am not a mixologist, I am a bartender." The straight-talking, straightforward founder of Schumann's bar in Munich, Germany, believes that when it comes to cocktail hour, keep it simple and elegant. "In a real cocktail bar, a man's outfit is very important," he says. "His clothes should be suitable for the evening. I've always said that I'd get to an age when I'd only wear suits, like Gianni Agnelli, and I've reached that age."

To recreate that elegant ambience – or at least its refreshments – at home, Mr Schumann, 71, maintains that "a couple of bottles of your favourite liquors are enough, but make sure they're premium quality. Gin and vodka allow you to make many different cocktails." His one rule for aspiring bartenders? "Never drink when you're behind the bar."

A veteran of the international institution that is Harry's Bar, Mr Schumann has been running his own establishment to much acclaim for more than 30 years. He even wrote a book, *American Bar*. So when is the proper cocktail hour? "The best hour is the blue hour – the hour after work finishes is the best time to have a cocktail, particularly after a really bad day or when you're with a very nice lady."

## CLARITO MARIA (THE CLASSIC COCKTAIL)
*You will need:*
2 oz English gin
A dash of Campari
A dash of Carpano Antica Formula
1 lime twist
*Method:*
Pour liquids into a cocktail shaker and stir.
Strain into a very cold Martini glass and add the lime twist.

## CHARLES DAIQUIRI (FOR THE LADIES)
*You will need:*
¼ oz lemon juice
¼ to ¾ oz sugar syrup
1½ oz white rum
¼ oz dark rum
1 slice of lime peel
*Method:*
Shake ingredients over ice cubes in a cocktail shaker.
Strain into a chilled cocktail glass and add the lime peel.

## MR PORTER (OUR OWN COCKTAIL)
*You will need:*
¼ oz Six Grapes port
¼ oz Schumann's Port (Niepoort port – late bottled vintage 1996)
A dash of orange bitter
1 tsp powdered sugar
champagne
*Method:*
Shake or stir all ingredients except the champagne
and pour them into a champagne flute.
Slowly pour in the champagne to fill the flute.

# THE LOOK

# MR JASON SUDEIKIS

*The* Saturday Night Live *comic on winning Oscars,
Wilde encounters and death by Jacuzzi*

WHILE MR JASON SUDEIKIS insists that he has "never had any kind of career plan", happily going "from vine to vine, taking whatever comes", he does have one absolutely non-negotiable goal. "I'm going to win an Oscar at 50 – definitely," he announces, his already deep voice dropping an extra half-octave for emphasis. "And I'm going to die at 49 and a half to ensure I get that Oscar. I need to die as close to the Oscar ceremony as possible so I'm the last person in the montage of dead people they show every year. That's the best spot, you know."

Has he planned how he'll die as precisely as when? "Oh definitely. It'll be in a hot tub, with my entire head squeezed into a jet. The photos are going to be hilarious. Man, I really hope the internet sticks around so people can reference this article in my obituaries and see that what sounds like a joke was actually amazingly prescient."

Aside from Jacuzzi-based death and a posthumous Oscar, Mr Sudeikis' career path has not been quite as happenstance as he might suggest. In fact, it verges on the traditional, having started out at renowned comedy theatre The Second City in Chicago before getting hired to work on *Saturday Night Live* and then moving easily into films. It's the exact same path trod by Mr Dan Aykroyd, Mr Chris Farley and Ms Tina Fey, to name a few. Having starred in two successful films in 2011 (*Hall Pass* with Mr Owen Wilson and *Horrible Bosses* with Mr Jason Bateman), as well as making a high-profile appearance in the critically fêted TV show *Eastbound & Down*, Mr Sudeikis' image as "kind of a goofy guy", one who concedes only to "giving the appearance of being busy", looks at serious risk of being undermined by high-profile success.

We meet on a bright and cold Monday afternoon in a photographer's studio in Manhattan with spectacular views of the Hudson River. "Pretty great, huh?" says Mr Sudeikis, taking, somewhat dorkily, pictures of the view with his phone as we sit down by the window. He has just finished his shoot for MR PORTER a whole hour and a half early, unheard of when it comes to fashion shoots.

"Oh yeah, I was determined to win that prize and be the fastest fashion model ever," he says dryly. (He later admits that trying on clothes is "not my favourite part of the job", and seeing as he makes that confession while shrugging on an anorak and a battered rucksack, his profession to fashion ignorance does not seem like part of his easy-going self-deprecation, but rather God's honest truth.)

Mr Sudeikis has a laconic, relaxed manner, talking slow and walking slow, that doubtless comes from his being a Midwesterner rather than a New Yorker, having grown up in Kansas. But mentally, he says, he has always had the kind of jittery and hyperactive curiosity that is a better reflection of his fast-moving career than his laid-back demeanour.

"I didn't want to be an actor when I was growing up – I wanted to be whatever I was reading about or seeing at the time. When I read *The Firm* I wanted to be a lawyer; when I saw *Top Gun*, I wanted to be a fighter pilot. So that's why acting probably turned out to be a good thing for me because I get to be different people for five minutes or 90 minutes. I'd be curious to see if I had the attention span to be like those guys on *30 Rock* and play the same character season after season," he says, as if unable even to imagine having a non-acting job that lasted for life as opposed to several seasons.

"Although there were two careers that did really interest me as a kid," he continues. "I wanted to be a basketball player, and when

I realised that wasn't a real thing, I wanted to be Axel Foley [Mr Eddie Murphy's character in *Beverly Hills Cop*]." So you were a white kid in Kansas who wanted to be black, I say. "Absolutely. And I see nothing unrealistic about that." Mr Sudeikis' ultimate decision to reject being Axel Foley in favour of being an actor was based, some might say, on equally unrealistic expectations, but ones that bore out. Mr Sudeikis' uncle is Mr George Wendt, aka Norm from *Cheers*, who is also a graduate of The Second City.

"Having George as an uncle made acting seem like a viable career. He met his wife at Second City so I looked at him and thought, wow, this Second City place, you go there, you marry a beautiful woman and you get a job on *Cheers* – sounds magical!" And that is near enough what happened to Mr Sudeikis, as he did meet his wife (now ex-wife), TV writer and producer Ms Kay Cannon, there and moved seamlessly to *Saturday Night Live*.

Mr Sudeikis has been frequently linked to various actresses by the celebrity press, from Ms January Jones to Ms Jennifer Aniston to one Olsen sister or another. He is currently dating Ms Olivia Wilde but the interest in his romantic life is one part of the job that makes him even more uncomfortable than trying on clothes. "Yeah, I don't really…" he begins, lost for words for the first time in an hour. "Uh, it is a little odd being chased around [by the press]. Fortunately all of the stories about me have been very flattering, but it is weird to read stories that are completely untrue and you think, 'Where did this come from? Who is this source?' Like, there was a story that Jennifer Aniston and I were dating. Obviously she's dealt with it for years so she's as cool as a cucumber about the whole thing but I'm like, 'How did they even come up with that?' It's weird, and it would be easy to let it make you close up as a person, but you have to choose not to be that way." He pauses for a second. "You know, I think those magazines should hire me because I think I'd be really good at writing those articles. I'm pretty intuitive and good at making insinuations."

And just like that, a new career plan is born.

# 10 DESIGNS FOR THE CUTTING-EDGE HOME

*We pick the best from Milan's annual
Salone Del Mobile design fair*

MILAN'S SALONE DEL MOBILE is the world's biggest design fair. And despite austerity measures and a wobbly euro, it continues to get bigger and bouncier every year. It can seem as if every major and minor design manufacturer, and indeed design student, is in attendance, as well as a number of car brands and other interested parties. The local fashion houses increasingly want a piece of the action too, either commissioning new furniture designs – as was the case with Hermès and Marni, among others – or giving store space over to new designs.

The design A-list – Ms Patricia Urquiola, Mr Konstantin Grcic, the collective Nendo and a dozen others – had designs produced by different manufacturers dotted around the city. Seeing it all is impossible and identifying trends is tricky.

There is, though, a definite emphasis on natural materials and sustainable production. The craftsman and the maker are very much the heroes of the hour, and most of the big names want to talk about the making as much as the design. The design world's relationship with "luxury" is complex and a little fraught, but there are definitely high-end materials aplenty, especially marble. There are crowd pleasers – Ms Urquiola never disappoints – and more conceptual experiments, with Nendo and Mr Ron Gilad as interested in the spaces design occupies, and how space contains it, as producing functional objects or tools for living.

In 2012, there were recognisable stools and sofas, shelving systems, cookers cleverer than you, and of course chairs. Some of them even looked quite comfy.

I

## "Medici" chair by Mr Konstantin Grcic for Mattiazzi

He might operate out of a nondescript studio in an unfashionable part of an unfashionable German city, among the kebab shops of Munich's Turkish quarter, but Mr Konstantin Grcic is the most admired and influential designer of the moment. His designs are functional, edgy, sometimes a little sharp-elbowed but usually more interesting and compelling than anything else on offer. While he is known as a committed industrial designer, Mr Grcic started out as a cabinet-maker; the "Medici" chair for Italian woodwork specialist Mattiazzi is, then, a sort of return to his roots, but it is

not like any wooden chair you have seen before, making full use of the Italian company's craftsmen and digital production techniques. The "Medici" is available in American walnut, Douglas fir and thermo-treated ash.

## 2
## "Tobi-Ishi" table by Barber Osgerby for B&B Italia

After designing the Olympic torch, Messrs Edward Barber and Jay Osgerby have joined Sir Jonathan Ive on the list of designers the British public might have heard of. Their first piece for B&B Italia, which takes its name from the ornamental stones in Japanese gardens, has a wooden top, polyurethane legs and a cement grout finish that makes it appear as three monolithic forms – a Stonehenge upgrade perhaps. It flirts with resembling a prop from the original *Star Trek*, but does enough to come off as strangely powerful – and definitely daring.

## 3
### "Const" lamp by Ms Ploypan Theerachai of Thinkk Studio

The "Const" lamp, from Bangkok-based Thinkk Studio, represents the best of 2012's Salone. An adjustable desk light reduced to three simple, assemble-yourself elements, it is both playful and ingenious, it smartly matches material and colour, and has an essential honesty. It does exactly what it needs to do, including keeping your pencils in order, in the simplest, most elegant way.

## 4
### "Pen" USB memory stick by Big-Game for Praxis

Big-Game, a Lausanne-based design trio, had a very good Salone 2012. Rather than po-faced minimalism, its designs are pared-down but always fun and engaging and, in Praxis, a Hong Kong-based maker of directional desk accessories, it has found the perfect partner. The Pen range of USB memory sticks are big, bright, beautiful and unforgettable.

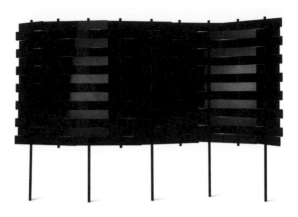

5

"Weave" screen by Nendo for K%

Japanese designer Mr Oki Sato, founder of design collective Nendo, was hard to escape at Salone in 2012. Mr Sato is having a moment and making the most of it. That's not to say he isn't still coming up with the goods. Among 2012's flurry of activities was the launch of new brand K%, for which Mr Sato is art director, from Singaporean design company K Projects. Its inaugural collection, "Black & Black" – a colour that Mr Sato has almost claimed as his own – is perhaps a more accessible take on his sharp-edged abstraction. And there's more to his "Weave" screen than to many of his designs.

6

"Rocky" credenza by Mr Charles Kalpakian for La Chance

Reviews for Mr Tom Dixon's "Most", a new Salone sideshow held at the Museum of Science and Technology, were mixed to say the least (though it was very popular with Milanese families who normally have to pay to play with the museum's trains, planes and submarines). But the debut appearance there by La Chance, established

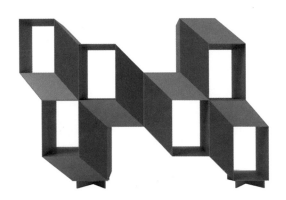

by a pair of twentysomething Parisians, did impress. Each piece in the collection appeared in two versions, poppy and bright or muted and severe, in line with the founders' belief that design buyers fall into those two camps. A particular favourite was the "Rocky" credenza by Beirut-born, Bagnolet-based designer Mr Charles Kalpakian, which is an op-arty treat.

## 7
### Colour porcelain by Scholten & Baijings for 1616 Arita

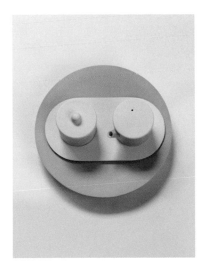

Dutch design duo Scholten & Baijings colluded with porcelain manufacturers 1616 Arita, a venerable Japanese company that has drafted in much-respected designer Mr Teruhiro Yanagihara as its creative director to liven things up. The result was a series of dinner services (a team of dishes previously side-lined by Ikea but making a comeback).

Arita is known for its superbly painted porcelain, and Sholten & Baijings layer the company's trademark colours on the simplest of shapes to dazzling effect. Each of the three services in the series enjoys a different degree of decoration ranging from "Minimal" to "Colourful" and "Extraordinary".

8
"Signs" coat stand by Big-Game for Karimoku New Standard

Established in 1940, Karimoku is one of Japan's leading makers of wooden furniture. In 2009 it brought in Mr Yanagihara and asked him to recruit international peers to produce designs under the Karimoku New Standard banner. Showing at the Brera district's lovely Erastudio Apartment Gallery, its 2012 collection was one of the hits of the fair, with total charmers from Mr Yanagihara and Mr Tomás Alonso. Big-Game's contribution included "Signs", a coat stand that performs a sort of semaphore and snaps back to being straight and narrow when not in use.

### 9
### "Compass Direction" desk by Mr Jean Prouvé, reissued by Vitra and G-Star

With the best back catalogue in the business, Vitra has a reputation for respectfully reissuing modern and modernist classics, but also having the confidence to know when and how to tweak and twist them for a contemporary audience. So when denim brand G-Star decided it might like to try its hand at putting out artful updates of classic pieces by the legendary French designer Mr Jean Prouvé, inevitably it turned to Vitra. In 2011, after two years of negotiations with the Prouvé family, the nine-strong Prouvé RAW collection was launched. At Salone, two more pieces were added, including "Compass Direction", all the desk any steel-disciplined modernist could ask for.

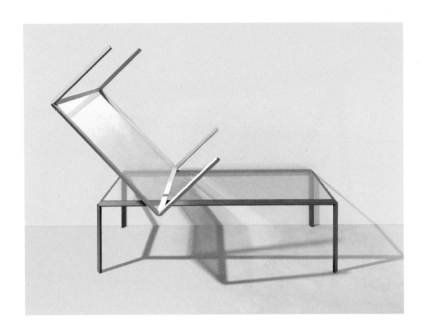

10

"Tavolino" coffee table by Mr Ron Gilad for Molteni & C

Mr Ron Gilad insists his designs "sit on the fat, delicious line between the abstract and the functional". And we're not going to argue. Mr Gilad is a designer with a philosophical bent, designing and thinking about what design actually is at the same time. His Grado° collection of tables, cabinets, bookcases and more for Italian company Molteni & C look like a series of line drawings; abstract geometry, as much nothing as something. "Tavolino" could definitely handle your coffee though.

# MEN OF NOTE
## DIPLO

*The roof-raising DJ and producer delves into his record bag*
*to pick the perfect Ibiza playlist for* MR PORTER

## "Discopolis"
### LIFELIKE & KRIS MENACE

"A tune that's before my time on the island, but the vibe (the video was shot in Ibiza) is of a sweet Barcelona chick drifting off into ecstasy at a villa."

## "G.O.M.H."
### REDLIGHT

"'Get Out My Head' – a crazy tune with the same percussive organ as 'Show Me Love', but enough aggression to make you jump up and down."

## "Save the World"
### SWEDISH HOUSE MAFIA

"This tune has everlasting appeal with its gigantic chorus and feel-good mentality."

## "Tung"
### DENIZ KOYU

"The siren horn, big sweeps and bass-line loop: this is a big tune right here – I use a special version I made with vocals in our Major Lazer live carnival."

## "Feel So Close"
### CALVIN HARRIS

"This song says, 'Hug me, I'm ecstatic'. From the warm guitar chords to the vocals, he's that big bro who wants you to have a good time. Let's party!"

"I Follow Rivers"

LYKKE LI

"Ibiza DJs are known for winding-down, post-dawn sets. This is perfect for when you want to just sit in a chair by a pool. Your mind can sing along – it works."

"Weekend"

MICHAEL GRAY

"This is a song that people request all the time and I thought would be fitting for this list."

# MR VINCENT KARTHEISER

*The stylish* Mad Men *actor on why he has more in common
with his TV character, Pete Campbell, than
you might imagine*

A COUPLE OF YEARS AGO, in 2010, Mr Vincent Kartheiser, who plays Pete Campbell in *Mad Men*, was telling interviewers about his somewhat eccentric, minimalist lifestyle. He didn't want children for environmental reasons, he said, and he had given away most of his possessions. He travelled by bus because he didn't own a car.

"Yeah, not any more," he says, with a shrug. "I own a car. I won't tell you which kind, but it's below $25,000, and it's a manual. I'm changing my own gears buddy!"

We're at a table outside Starbucks on a busy intersection on Sunset Boulevard, a strangely exposed and public place to meet, particularly for the star of a huge TV show. But Mr Kartheiser doesn't view himself as a star. And he doesn't behave like one either. Certainly, to turn so firmly against materialism is rare in any celebrity, let alone one who plays an executive at a Madison Avenue advertising agency, one of the engines of consumerism.

"I know. But I'm just a regular dude now."

The minimalism thing is over?

"Until it comes back, yeah," he says. "I'm an extremist. I go through weird phases that I fully believe in at the time. Then of course, six months later I have to back step." He puts on a voice. "Gee, sorry folks, I don't believe in that stuff much any more… "

He sounds like a character from *Looney Tunes*.

"Well I am kind of *Looney Tunes*, this one." He points at himself. "But see, everyone changes – if you don't change between 26 and 33, then you haven't been trying. It's just most of us don't give interviews about it. So my big lesson is to just not talk about it in interviews. And that's hard for me, because I tend to be an open book. It's like going against my nature."

This is certainly true. We're only a few minutes in, and already he might be one of the most frank and revealing people – let alone celebrities – that I've ever met. He has a bright, animated way about him, a shade louder than most perhaps. He doesn't just respond to questions, but gives the truest answer he can, and if that means exposing his own vulnerabilities in the process, then so be it. It may be what makes him such a compelling actor, this ability to not only access instantly the kind of thoughts and emotions that many of us might classify "innermost", but then express them articulately and without reservation to strangers.

For instance, when I ask him what he has in common with Pete Campbell, he doesn't flinch: "A whole lot!" It's not the most obvious answer, given that Campbell has been described as preppy, oily, insecure, scheming and ruthless. But Mr Kartheiser doesn't care.

"He's perpetually unsatisfied, and that's a trait I share," he says. "Peter is a little man, and so am I. Little physically, but also in the game. Remember, a lot of our similarities come down to the creator, Matthew Weiner, knowing his actors. He writes to people's strengths. So he might look at me and say, 'Oh Vinny has an inferiority complex'. Well Pete has one too!"

There's a kind of symbiosis between characters and cast and how the two evolve. Certainly Don Draper's strength and stature are mirrored by Mr Jon Hamm on set, just as Campbell's insecurity is reflected in Mr Kartheiser.

"Don't get me wrong, I get along terribly well with the cast," he says. "I don't think they hate me as much as they hate Pete Campbell, but maybe I worry that they do. So I share that with Pete."

That's a very frank admission.

"And Pete Campbell is very frank! He says things that are socially awkward but f***ing true, and I do that a lot. I'm saying these things to you now and I know I'll get calls from cast members saying, 'Dude, do you think I hate you? Stop telling people that. I might hate you if you say that again'."

The clearest parallel between the two men is more profound. Mr Kartheiser was 26 when he joined the cast of *Mad Men*, just as Campbell was when he joined Sterling Cooper. And over the past seven years, both men have matured, made money and achieved great success in their careers, an experience that has changed them in unexpected ways. While Campbell went from account executive to partner, a position he once craved but now finds unfulfilling, Mr Kartheiser rose from relative obscurity to starring in one of the most acclaimed shows on television. But his disillusion is the same.

"It's like Oscar Wilde said: 'There are two great tragedies in life'," he says. "'One is not getting what you want, and the other is getting it.'"

There's no question that Mr Kartheiser has got what he always wanted. He started acting at the age of six, in local theatre in Minneapolis, and found success as a regular on the TV series *Angel* for a few years. But *Mad Men* was different. He knew instantly that it was a special project – he's likened it to a Russian novel in its complexity and subtext, and he has only the highest praise for Messrs Weiner and Hamm.

And like Pete Campbell, success isn't as he imagined it as a younger man. "Teenagers have a much clearer perspective of who they are than when they're 30, you know?" he says. "A teenager can say, 'I really believe in animals, and I want to be a veterinarian and you should pursue your dreams…' But most people, when they grow up, they're like, 'f*** animals. And f*** your dreams! My dreams got s*** on, so will yours!' They stop being the pure colours they once were and turn into these stomped-out shadows of who they thought they would be."

What sort of a person did you think you would become?

"I thought I'd be an adult!" He looks outraged, as though he's been robbed. "I remember looking at 30 year olds and thinking, 'He smells like an adult, the things he does are adult'. But now I realise that they're just teenagers who got older. You might do adult things like shave your face and pay your taxes, but you have a lot of the same insecurities, a lot of the same socially awkward abilities and, um, not-awkward abilities."

We both notice the irony that he said that last part awkwardly. But I don't want to mention it. It might be awkward.

"I think in America we just look at people's careers and assume they're happy," he continues. "So it can be difficult to then get rid of the idea that professional success will complete me."

These days, Mr Kartheiser isn't even pursuing success in the conventional sense. He avoids late-night talk shows and the interview circuit. He doesn't chase big movie roles, preferring instead to make tiny, experimental independent films.

"Eventually," he says, "you start coming to terms with the fact that maybe we're not meant to feel complete at all." And with that, he gets up to leave. The interview doesn't feel complete. But that's probably just as well.

# KNITTED TIES

*No longer the preserve of university lecturers,*
*these are now a neat modern style staple*

KNITTED TIES are characterised by their textured, loosely woven appearance, absence of a lining (hold one up to the light and it will shine through) and slightly springy feel. The French term *cri de la soie*, which translates as "the cry of silk", is sometimes used to describe the crisp, crunchy sound that knitted ties make when they are squeezed in the hand. Most have blunt ends (as opposed to the pointed tips found on conventional neckties), and they can be knitted from both silk and wool, with the latter type best suited to autumn and winter. From Ivy Leaguers and the silver screen to runway shows, the knitted tie is a stylish – and often underrated – wardrobe component, one that will add individuality to your look while keeping things classic.

## WHEN TO WEAR A KNITTED TIE

Knitted ties are at the less formal end of the neckwear spectrum and can be deployed to dress down a suit or to dress up a casual outfit. You wouldn't wear one to a board meeting, but they come into their own when you are off duty, for example teamed with a button-down shirt, chinos and a blazer at a casual wedding. They are perfect for "smart-casual" dress codes – when you want to wear a tie but suspect others may not: you won't be overdressed, even if everyone else is without a tie. They are also great for travelling, as they won't crease.

A block-colour knitted tie works well with a patterned shirt,
as Mr Alexander Skarsgård in 2011 demonstrates

### THE KNOT

The most appropriate knot for knitted ties is the basic four-in-hand.
The textured surface (as a result of the knitted fabric) means that
any chosen knot will be noticeably larger than on a conventional silk
tie. With this in mind, it makes sense to use the smallest type of knot
to avoid the unappealing overstuffed look. Don't be afraid to tighten
the knot firmly to achieve a desirable size. Also, the slightly unsym-
metrical shape of the four-in-hand knot complements the less
formal nature of the knitted tie.

Mr Darren McGavin on the set of *The Night Stalker*, 1975

### THE LENGTH

Since they are less formal, knitted ties can be worn slightly shorter than their regular counterparts (they need not quite reach the waistband), and also with the rear blade longer than the front blade for a carefree, individualistic look. The open weave of knitted ties makes them more susceptible to stretching, so they should be stored rolled up rather than on a hanger. Some manufacturers make their knitted ties slightly shorter than their regular ties to account for the small amount of natural stretch that will occur even with proper care.

As Mr Michael Hill of Drake's puts it, "there's a touch of sartorial audacity in a silk knitted tie". Keep this in mind when constructing an outfit. Consider wearing the knot slightly loose, or having the rear blade longer than the front one. Knitted ties can add a touch of *sprezzatura* to your look. They are also great for adding texture and visual interest, and block-colour ties go with most shirt and jacket patterns and combinations. A knitted tie, for instance, unites a tweed jacket and a tattersall shirt, without having to find a tie in a third pattern that will match.

## OR FOR A MORE FORMAL LOOK...

Knitted ties bear a passing resemblance to grenadine ties, but the two types should not be confused. Grenadine ties are textured like knitted ties, but to a lesser degree. Their weave is tighter, and they have an interlining as well as pointed ends. This means that grenadine ties are more formal than their knitted counterparts: they can be worn in most situations where you would wear a standard silk necktie (although Sir Sean Connery demonstrates the power of a relaxed, loose knot).

Sir Sean Connery, seen here on the set of *Dr No* in 1962,
wears a silk grenadine tie with aplomb

# MR ALLEN LEECH

*Meet the young actor, who stars as* Downton Abbey's
*rebel Irishman*

WHEN I POST on my Twitter account that I am about to interview Mr Allen Leech – widely known to audiences as Tom Branson, the chauffeur-turned-estate manager in the hit TV series *Downton Abbey*, who seduced and married one of the ladies of the manor – the reactions range from swooning to downright jealousy. While the award-winning historical drama has attracted a cult following, it seems that Mr Leech has become something of a heart-throb. If he is aware of this fact, however, it is something that he wears lightly. Classically handsome and with an easy-going manner, Mr Leech is bemused when I ask him if he has heard of a website called F\*\*k Yeah Allen Leech, on which die-hard *Downton* fans have posted stills of Branson, many lovingly annotated with his lines from the show ("I promise to devote every waking minute to your happiness").

Although Mr Leech has appeared in two other historical dramas (HBO's *Rome* in 2007 and Showtime's *The Tudors* in 2010), he has a diverse set of films, TV shows and theatre productions under his belt. In *The Sweeney* he played Simon Ellis, a member of a brutal-but-effective elite police squad – a world apart from the fanciful costumes and cut-glass accents of *Downton*.

Meanwhile, Mr Leech describes the time he spent in 2011 starring in Mr Mike Leigh's West End production *Ecstasy* as "One of the most enjoyable experiences I have had professionally".

*Did you miss Branson's chauffeur outfit, when he ceased to be a member of staff in the third series?*
I did miss it, actually. Mainly because it gave me a real sense of the character's identity when I put it on, and there was a ritual to getting into the garters, the green jacket, the goggles and all that stuff. But I finally got to wear other outfits, which was great... I mean, I spent two years as an oversized leprechaun, so it was nice to get into some tuxedos. *Downton* is set in the early 1900s, and because Branson is the guy who is against the establishment he is the first character to rock up in a tux rather than in full tails, so I had some of the sharpest gear to wear.

*Are there any characters you've played whose outfits have influenced your personal style?*
Well, the jacket I'm wearing right now is from *The Sweeney* so I guess I have! Not always, though. For [the 2003 film] *Cowboys & Angels* there was this red leather jacket, and as a joke I brought it out and said, "What about this for my character?" and of course it turned out it actually was his jacket, but in the end it looked great on camera.

*Finally, I heard you had an unusual animal encounter while you were filming* Man About Dog...
I know what you want to know. In the film there was a scene where I was sleeping on a bed beside a greyhound and I had to keep the dog calm so we could get the shot. I'm not going to lie, the way I had to do it was by massaging the dog's balls! It's true, and I'm not ashamed of it... although I hope never to have to do it again. The things you do for the business. The funniest thing was the dog handler on set, who said, "Personally, I find one of the best ways to keep a dog calm in bed is to..." and I was like, "Hang on a minute! How many times have you found yourself in bed with a dog needing to be kept calm? Is this a problem you often encounter?"

# THE KNACK
# (AND HOW TO GET IT)

*MR PORTER's regular feature,
in which experts offer practical advice
on a variety of subjects, from the
celebratory to the artistic, via the sartorial*

# THE KNACK

# HOW TO APPRECIATE JAZZ

*By Mr Terence Blanchard, multiple Grammy
Award-winning jazz musician and composer*

I FELL IN LOVE with jazz as a kid when I realised that the trumpet could bend notes like a human voice. When I became a teenager, I learnt how expressive the music was. It allows one's own voice to speak. Growing up in New Orleans, I heard the traditional forms of jazz which I could compare to modern forms of the music from my record collection. This made me realise how the music could evolve and it stimulated my curiosity for how I could contribute person-ally. People can appreciate jazz because of its honest look at life. The music was created from the bowels of American history. When you consider the swing era, you get a true depiction of the time period in which it was made as much as you do when you listen to the more modern and groundbreaking period of the 1960s. Any true art is a reflection of the time it was created, and jazz is no exception.

## 01
### BE OPEN MINDED

Not everyone wears a black beret or cool hat (although big mechanical watches and sleek eyeglasses work rather well). It's not all easy listening or hard or edgy. Jazz is dynamic; it can be traditional, modern and avant-garde, all in the same tune. In order to appreciate jazz, you have to open your heart, your mind and your soul.

## 03
### IDENTIFY THE INSTRUMENTS

Try to listen to every instrument and pick out their role in the song. Ask yourself how the drummer's beats are controlling the pace. Listen to the bass, how does it fit into the song? Follow the trumpet, is that shaping the tune? Is the piano filling in empty spaces or adding depth? A jazz band is like a locomotive with an engine, steam, wheels and tracks. All of the parts make it move.

## 02

### RELAX AND ENJOY

If you're visiting a jazz club, sit down, order a cocktail, enjoy the room and check out the band. If the music moves you, clap your hands, sway your body, get up and dance. No one is going to tell you to stop.

## 04

### FEEL THE MUSIC

Try to pick out pairings of instruments and see how they are communicating, passing musical ideas back and forth. This is when you really get to know jazz. Is the drummer challenging the bass player who is driving the beat? On any given tune, we begin with a framework. Where we go with the groove and where we end up is all determined by the interplay or the improvisation. If you can follow this with your brain and soul, you will love jazz.

# SOME COMMON MISTAKES

### READING UP

People assume that you need to have a vast knowledge of jazz history to appreciate it. Jazz is based on emotion. It is democratic and everyone can share in it.

### BEING OVER TECHNICAL

You needn't know music theory. All you require is an open mind and an eagerness to experience the sounds of the instruments. Whether you can understand the rhythmic structure or not, the question is did it sound good, and did it make you smile? Just sit back, relax and allow your brain to follow the music.

### BAD ETIQUETTE

When at a jazz club, some people talk through a show as if it were background music. This is probably the worst thing for a jazz musician and disrespectful to other audience members. You do not have to be totally silent but try not to discuss global economic policy while the band are playing their hearts out.

### LETTING YOUR EYE WANDER

Don't go to a jazz concert with the sole intention of picking up women. Although I'm sure there have been many connections made at jazz concerts most people are there for the music. Jazz has an ability to open people up which makes a jazz club a good date destination. Just come out, hear some cool new music and have a good time.

# HOW TO BEHAVE IN A SPA

*By Mr Mansel Fletcher, who knows how to relax*

WHEN THE WOMAN in your life tells you she wants to spend a weekend in the country, bear in mind that most country-house hotels now come with spas attached. She's likely to believe that a trip to the spa is one of the weekend's vital components and it behoves a modern man to join in, even if he would rather, in truth, head for the bar in search of televised sport and a bottle of red wine. If spas are unfamiliar territory this guide will help you give the impression that you're sufficiently sophisticated to be entirely at ease.

## 01
### BE WILLING TO RELAX

Spa treatments are meant to be relaxing. This is why it makes more sense to have a treatment in a hotel – where afterwards you can pad to your room and lie down – than in an urban spa, where you're spat back into the bustle of city life.

## 02
### PREPARE YOURSELF

Show your therapist some respect by showering before your treatment, and remember to wear some underwear by which you're happy to be judged. And unless otherwise instructed, keep them on.

## 03
### SPEAK UP

If something hurts, or if your massage doesn't hurt enough, tell the therapist. What's torture for one man may merely tickle another. Also, if you suspect your skin is reacting badly to a product that's been applied, speak up sooner rather than later.

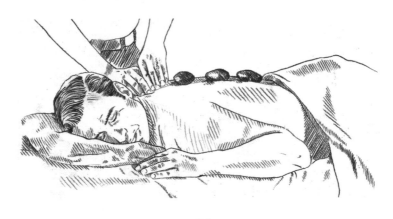

## 04
### GO TO SLEEP

How better to relax than with a nap? You may quibble that a man can have a relaxing snooze without spending money on a treatment, but the therapist's work will achieve the same results whether you're awake or asleep. Much of what's good about having a treatment is the enforced downtime.

## 05
### HAVE ANOTHER SHOWER AND DRINK SOME WATER

Spas are invariably warm, so drink some water at the end of the treatment to rehydrate. Also, whether you're having a facial or a massage, the chances are that your hair will end up coated in unguent. This should be washed out before you reach the dinner table, and (at last!) that well-deserved glass of red.

# SOME COMMON MISTAKES

## TOUCHING THE MASSEUSE

No, no, no. It's not that kind of massage. Who do you think you are, an ex-head of the International Monetary Fund?

## BEING TOO NAKED,
## OR NOT NAKED ENOUGH

You need to remove your trousers and your shirt. However, unless there's a very good reason to believe otherwise, your underwear stays on.

## FAILING TO EXPLAIN WHAT YOU WANT

If you want a rigorous sports massage then say so, to avoid being given nothing tougher than a back rub. Whatever it is you want, be clear – many spa treatments promise nothing more tangible than a sense of wellbeing.

## NOT KNOWING WHAT TO EXPECT

If in doubt, ask. MR PORTER has a friend who, while staying at an Aman resort, spent a lot of money on a massage to relieve the aches brought on by a week's skiing. He went for a reiki massage, but discovered too late that it was non-touching – the masseuse merely passed her hands over his body.

## FORGETTING YOUR SWIMMING TRUNKS

Will there be a pool? Or a sauna? Who knows, but it's always worth packing a pair of swimming shorts just in case.

# HOW TO BOND WITH
# YOUR FATHER-IN-LAW

*By Mr David Whitehouse*

LET'S NOT MINCE our words. You are sleeping with his daughter. That should frame this entire lesson in the required context – your relationship with the father of the woman you love will be the single most awkward in your life. You have just one thing in common: a desire not to anger his daughter. That is all. Despite this lack of shared ground you have to get on. Unfortunately this is statistically unlikely. You're of different generations, beliefs and interests. Regardless, you must try. You really have no other choice.

## 01
### PITCH IT RIGHT

You have a specific role to fulfil. You must be strong, but you are
not the alpha male. He is. Still, do not show weakness. Get ready
for a needlessly firm handshake and polite cough to mask the sound
of the metacarpophalangeal joints in your fingers crumbling to
a powder. By all means beat him at board games – it'll display the
dexterity of mind he'll demand from the man his daughter loves –
but if you must, do so by a sporting margin. In Monopoly, taking
him for all he's worth with your Mayfair hotel before bailing him
out using a 600% interest rate loan will not do. Remember your
place (below his).

## 02

### HAVE WHAT HE'S HAVING

Your father-in-law will never share your interests. Firstly, he's old. As men get older, their willingness to try new things stagnates, it doesn't matter how much you espouse the benefits of Zumba. Secondly, their comprehension of new technology will be limited. Tell him about your web design company all you like; you might as well try explaining Bluetooth to a cow. Thirdly, you're sleeping with his daughter. So do what he wants to do. You've broken your ankles kite surfing and he wants to go hill walking? Wrap up warm!

## 03

### PREPARE TO BE TESTED

This is a job interview, and you're going for the role of "Man Who Doesn't Want His Future to Feature a Miserable Old Bastard". You're going to need to be able to converse on any topic he might raise. If your partner was fathered by a man who lives for the heady world of wicker basket weaving, then embrace it with all the gusto you can muster. If he asks why birch bark baskets, commonly used throughout the subarctic, are often embellished with dyed porcupine quills, then you'd better hope you have an answer.

## 04
### MAKE FRIENDS WITH YOUR MOTHER-IN-LAW

Your new father-in-law wants to see hard evidence that his daughter's spouse knows how to treat a woman. Offering to go upstairs to help straighten her hair is overzealous. Instead, briefly turn your attention to the mother-in-law. If she can find a place for you in her affections, then he must too. That said, act in moderation. If she notes that a task needs doing, politely offer your assistance, thus demonstrating an endearing selflessness. This might include going to the shop or opening some more wine. It does not include standing outside the toilet and asking whether she's OK through the door.

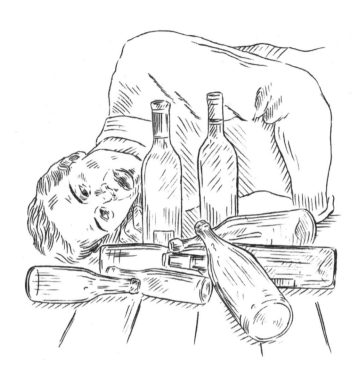

### STAY ON YOUR GUARD

Meeting the in-laws is a highly strung situation. Often, alcohol will be deployed as a social lubricant. Drink precisely 50% of the amount your father-in-law drinks. Outmoded thinking suggests that you should match him glass for glass, but this isn't the 1970s and you are not a professional darts player. Let him tell you how the evening has gone and do not allow a perceived success to distract you from your single-minded goal: leaving with your head held high, his daughter in your arms. If at the end of the night you're carrying him to bed and calling him dad, neither of you will find it particularly funny in the morning. But then, he's not the one that's trying to impress, is he?

# SOME COMMON MISTAKES

## LET FACTUAL INACCURACIES LIE

The worst thing you can do is be a pedant. If he lays claim to having served in Vietnam and giving Sir James Dyson the idea for his revolutionary vacuum cleaner, let him believe it. To try to shoot him down is to crash your own plane into the sea while taking aim.

## KNOW WHERE YOUR PARTNER'S LOYALTIES LIE

She might be in love with you, but that man over there, the one suggesting that you have the upper body of an eight-year-old Russian gymnast just because you've never played rugby sevens, is her father. She won't be impressed if you point out that he's an idiot, even if you are right.

## FORGIVE HIM

His overbearing, try-hard alpha-male posing might be annoying, or his powerfully boring talk of accounting methods might be tedious. But remember, one day your daughter will bring a man home. And if you're not boring by then, you'll certainly want to believe you can beat him in an arm wrestle.

# HOW TO DANCE AT A WEDDING

*By Mr David Whitehouse,*
*who knows how to move with the times*

WEDDINGS ARE TESTS of diplomacy at which a dance can be
an act of war. You must get it right. No other set of circumstances
brings together so many tenuously connected strangers, puts them
in a giant tent, fills them with wine and subjects them to the music
of Mr Chris de Burgh. If you dance – and you must dance – it will
likely be to music you loathe. By your side will be any combination of best friends, old enemies, loved ones, confused pension-
ers and hyperactive children, and you must adapt. What began as
a slow clinch with an amorous bridesmaid to the sensual tones of
Mr Marvin Gaye might devolve into doing "The Time Warp" with
a four year old. Unlike any other area of your life, the key here is to
try to please everyone.

## 01

### PICK YOUR MOMENT

This is a wedding, meaning the track list might as well have been chosen by a dog. Enter the floor to a song you like, or can at least bear, so you can find your groove before the DJ spins a tune so criminal it could be used to extract money from a bank. You need to stride in confidently, which won't happen if, halfway through your approach, they drop a Mr Phil Collins classic, forcing you to do the "Whoops, I forgot my wallet" shuffle back to your table.

## 02

### PLAY IT SAFE

No one ever danced well while drunk… but dancing at a wedding isn't about dancing well. Anything other than a conventional wedding shuffle singles you out as a show-off. Doing "the worm", for example, will confound the bride's parents. Dance humbly and with manners. This isn't a return to glory days of your clubbing youth. If you can't do it to the music of Abba, it has no place here.

## 03
### GRAB A PARTNER

Weddings are about coming together, and so you must. If the groom's grandmother, who's probably so old she's biologically closer to a tortoise than a human, wants to dance, you dance. If the bride's five-year-old niece insists that you drop to the floor for Dolly Parton's "Nine to Five", thus disintegrating the knees on your new suit trousers, you drop. The wedding dance is a utopia of sorts: it doesn't recognise age or ability. Work the room.

## 04
### KNOW WHEN TO STOP

This is a wedding, and the end of a wedding means one thing: the slow dance. This is a time for romance. Five minutes before this allotted time, take a second to (soberly) look around you. If you are not with a partner, staying on the floor means you must take one and hold them tenderly for the seemingly seven-hour duration of Ms Celine Dion's "My Heart Will Go On". Think carefully.

# HOW TO CREATE
# A BESPOKE BLOODY MARY

*By Mr Thomas Morris, senior bartender
at 45 Park Lane, London*

THE DELIGHTS OF alcohol, tomato juice and spice are an experience to be savoured. One might think these seemingly odd ingredients form a recipe for tragedy, a taste phenomenon that surely cannot constitute a cocktail. However, with the right methods and ingredients, there's nothing better.

Historical accounts of the true origins of this infamous Sunday morning concoction differ. In my humble opinion, true recognition should be credited to Mr Fernand "Pete" Petiot, a bartender in the 1920s who served up the first "Bloody" in Harry's New York Bar in Paris. Today, millions of aficionados have developed their own variations, recipes and additions, making the bespoke Bloody Mary an interesting weekend staple.

# THINGS YOU'LL NEED

## INGREDIENTS

2oz (60ml) vodka, 3½oz tomato juice, ½oz freshly squeezed
lemon juice, ice, Tabasco, Worcestershire sauce, basil leaf,
baby vine tomato, cayenne pepper sauce, horseradish,
ground black pepper, celery salt

## EQUIPMENT

16oz mixing glass, clean highball glass, hawthorne strainer,
bar spoon, jigger (to measure liquids), straws to garnish

## MIX WITH THE BEST

Pour a healthy measure (2oz; 60ml) of top-quality vodka (Belvedere or Chase are particularly good) into a 16oz mixing glass; add 3½oz of tomato juice and ½oz of freshly squeezed lemon juice. A jigger is the best thing to use for quantities.

02

## SOME LIKE IT HOT

As the tradition goes, add three dashes of Tabasco and six of Worcestershire sauce. Next, try individualising the Bloody Mary with different spices such as a pinch of celery salt and ground black pepper, one teaspoon of Atomic horseradish and two teaspoons of cayenne pepper sauce. The latter is one of my secret ingredients.

03
CHILL OUT

Cool the drink in its mixing glass with ice and use a bar spoon to mix the contents. Try not to mix for too long or you will dilute the drink. Using a hawthorne strainer, pour the contents from the mixing glass into a highball glass full of cubed ice. This tool will fine-strain the cocktail and keeps the liquid clear.

04
CROWN YOUR COCKTAIL

Variety and ingenuity rule supreme, meaning the garnish is the most essential part to finishing a bespoke Bloody Mary. Try adding a baby vine tomato, basil leaf and some black pepper dust to truly crown the creation. Slip in a straw and enjoy.

# SOME COMMON MISTAKES

### ALCOHOL IGNORANCE

Many people are tempted (especially if you are indulging in some hair of the dog therapy) to be over generous with the vodka. Similarly, some choose to use less. Measure this key ingredient carefully (60ml) to perfect the overall taste.

### A BAD MIX

You want your Bloody to be nice and cold, and you don't want to dilute your cocktail with melted ice. Mix the correct amount to achieve the optimum temperature for serving. Thirty revolutions of the ice using a bar spoon will do the trick.

### HIDING FROM THE HEAT

Don't be shy with experimenting to find the exact amount of Tabasco, hot sauce, horseradish and Worcestershire sauce to satisfy your palate.

### WRONG RECEPTACLE

There are many glasses to choose from, but one should always serve a Bloody Mary in a highball glass over ice. The highball is a classic, easy-to-drink-from vessel and it houses the ingredients perfectly. This completes a refreshing, chilled cocktail to enjoy with your Sunday brunch.

### BEING DULL

Some people are afraid to think outside the box. Luckily for all, there is no such thing as wrong when making a bespoke Bloody Mary. Add anything you think might enhance your experience.

# HOW TO DRESS FOR
# A FESTIVAL

*By Mr David Whitehouse, festival pro*

STYLE AND FESTIVALS are old adversaries. The likelihood is
you're sleeping in a tent, which is hopefully the closest you'll come
to living in a bin. Gone are home comforts. Your mirror is the foil
in a cigarette carton. Your bathtub is a wet wipe. Your wardrobe is
the scrunched up contents of a badly packed bag. And then there's
the weather. The weather hates you. If it wasn't so good at
creating the finely tuned ecosystems that sustain all life on
earth, we'd abolish it. And if you're going to spend all day in it,
listening to music or queuing for three hours to get your hands on
a hotdog the hue of Mr Johnny Depp's skin in *Edward Scissorhands*,
the odds of you looking good are slim. So better to follow the rules.

## BID GOODBYE TO YOUR COMFORT ZONE

Want to look exactly as you wish? Stay at home. Things are different here. For example, sewage systems aren't considered a basic human right. Festival style is a heady blend of the untamed with the functional, the beautiful with the necessary. Flesh and wellies. Perfume and sun tan lotion. Canada Goose parka and shorts. Embrace it. The guy in the corner with the pressed shirt, brogues and the well-cut trousers? He's the anomaly. No, worse, he's the party pooper.

## 02

## MASTER THE ART OF CAMOUFLAGE

Successful festival dressing is largely about disguise. The trick is to create a character, a sun-kissed alter ego who can dance, outside, at one in the afternoon, without feeling the crippling weight of self-consciousness. Embrace largesse. That's not to say you need approach it as if you're RuPaul at Rio Carnival, but unless you go bold on colours and accessories at a festival you're going to look like a grumpy mime artist trapped in an episode of *Teletubbies*.

## 03
### BE COOL

You really must remember the festival fundamentals. Sunglasses and a hat that can cover the eyes, a Hartford trilby or Paul Smith Panama say, are (almost) more essential than water. Whatever you do, don't combine said hat with a wife-beater vest and a jeer – this is the most snoring of festival uniforms and the exact opposite of what those men that do adopt this look are so desperately seeking – cool.

## 04
### NEVER GIVE UP

It's only rain. OK, so sartorially it is a tricky situation – nobody ever wore a transparent plastic poncho without looking like the used prophylactic of a giant whale. However, the other extreme reaction to heavy rainfall is a similarly bad scene. Anyone seen abandoning clothes and bathing in mud deserves to get diseases commonly found in pigs. The weather can be styled out. Ponchos, trench foot or arrest, however, cannot.

## 05
### (NOT) WITH THE BAND

Certain looks are guaranteed at any festival the world over. They form in clusters, much like acne. There will always be women slavishly devoted to the Mses Kate Moss/ Sienna Miller boho-chic of Glastonbury 2001-2005, though they will invariably bear a closer resemblance to an inexpensive lampshade. Equally criminal are those men that opt to dress as if they're in a band playing the festival. Under no circumstances attempt this. The reason that Kings of Leon, for example, are able to dress like that at festivals is because they get ferried around in golf carts and helicopters. In normal situations even they look ridiculous. If it says The Ramones on your T-shirt, you'd better have been in them.

# SOME COMMON MISTAKES

### SANDALS

No matter how hot it is, sandals at festivals are for people who like to walk home barefoot and with broken toes. You don't have hooves.

### ADULT ROMPER SUIT

You wouldn't wear a massive fluorescent phallus with a huge flashing red arrow pointing right down at your face, would you? No? Just checking.

### BUYING THINGS AT FESTIVALS

Yeah, those friendship bracelets were a good idea, bought while you were of sound mind. As was that tattoo.

## THE KNACK
# HOW TO GET OUT OF A HAIR RUT

*By Mr Matt Mulhall, hair stylist*

FOR THE MAJORITY of us, breaking free from a hairstyle we've adopted since our late teens is an uncomfortable proposition. "Men tend to stick to the same styles because of their liking for familiarity," says Mr Matt Mulhall, who has been maintaining the manes of London's most influential men for more than 23 years. "They think they know what works, but as the years go by styles change and they can be left looking out of touch and older than their years." Mr Mulhall, who also coifs the hair of models at menswear shows including Lanvin and Burberry, has imparted some of his wisdom to help men climb out of their hair rut.

## 01
### THE CRITIQUE

Before you head in for your next cut, take a good, long look at yourself in the mirror and think about what you like and dislike about your hair. Be honest. Like your skin, your hair ages and its style should adjust with your years. Trying to stave off ageing with a mid-life mohawk is not advisable. If you are still unsure and want to see your hair the way others see it, take a photo or shoot a short video so you can see the back and sides.

## 02
### PICK YOUR CUT

Once you have thoroughly assessed yourself, gather up some reference material by leafing through some men's fashion magazines, looking at the advertising campaigns of brands you think are stylish and age-appropriate. It's also worthwhile paying attention to smart men around you and scrutinising how they style their hair. Don't get overwhelmed – sometimes just a few small changes can make a world of difference to how you feel and are perceived.

## 03
### CHANGE YOUR HAIRDRESSER

Picking the right hairdresser is important. Ideally, you need to find someone who is on your wavelength and understands what you want and, perhaps more importantly, what will suit you. The best way of discovering who fits your needs is asking around and doing research. Don't be frightened to make enquiries with friends. Contrary to common opinion, this won't make you a freak. If you are forking out on a cut every four weeks you should be using someone you like and who delivers your requirements.

## 04
### DRESS THE PART

Your hairdresser responds to your character and the manner in which you present yourself, so it's wise to turn up looking the way you want to look, rather than how you happen to look straight out of bed. Make the effort and don't arrive wearing your sloppy Saturday sweatpants.

Information is one of the most important things when it comes to getting a haircut. Don't clam up and just say, "What do you think?" Similarly, if you are happy with the result and want to know how it's achieved, don't be shy about asking your hairdresser to explain which shampoo to use, whether you need conditioner, or for a step-by-step routine on how to style your hair with the products.

## SOME COMMON MISTAKES

### BEING PERSISTANT

One of the most frequent complaints I hear from the barber's chair is, "My hair texture seems to have changed." That's probably because it has. Hair changes as we age so it's futile attempting to keep a hairstyle that was first cut during the flush of youth. It wasn't the hairstyle that made you anyway; it was the stress-free countenance.

### KEEPING IT (UN)REAL

Be realistic with the capabilities and abundance of your hair. If it's thinning at the front, chances are you won't be able to achieve a large quiff.

### BEING "ON-TREND"

Hair is one area in your life where transient looks are best avoided. Keep it masculine, keep it classic. Mid-life is not the right time to get a statement haircut or colour. A short back and sides has been around for a long time for good reason: it looks great at any age.

# HOW TO HIT THE GROUND RUNNING

*By Mr Mansel Fletcher, business travel aficionado*

MR GEORGE CLOONEY'S character in the movie *Up in the Air* may have been the first man in history who didn't find regular business travel a drag. It's not just a drag because it's impossible to solicit any sympathy from friends or family who don't travel for work – they invariably imagine that every time a man steps on an aeroplane he's going on holiday – but because travel can take its toll on a guy. Between the early starts, the endless hours spent in airless environments and the temptation to subsist on a diet that consists of coffee and carbs during the day, and rich food and drink in the evening, it's hard to look, or feel, your best. Our advice? By combining diligent use of some essential grooming products with a thoughtful approach to one's health, a man can be assured that not only will he win the business, he'll also look the business.

## 01
### PERFECT YOUR PACKING

While it's a virtue to travel light, it's more important to be well prepared. We suggest, for a three-night trip, one blue suit, a pair of khaki chinos that can be worn with the suit jacket for more casual meetings, two knitted ties (they won't crease in a suitcase), one pair of black Oxfords and one pair of brown loafers. If you want to change for dinner then pack two shirts and two sets of underwear for each day. Gym kit is also recommended – with the family out of the equation, you've got no excuses for dodging the treadmill.

## 02
### SOME PRE-FLIGHT PREP

To ensure the long haul doesn't dull your sartorial edge, prepare yourself accordingly. Firstly, take a suit carrier. There's never enough space in the steward's hanging closet, so in order to save your suit, place the jacket in your carrier before you get onto the plane and store it flat in an overhead compartment. Secondly, moisturise. Air conditioning hates you. And while we're not advising doing this proudly in front of fellow passengers, discreetly topping up when you head to the toilet will keep you looking perky.

## 03
### PACK THE RIGHT KIT

A good Dopp kit should contain all the grooming essentials for the modern-day gentleman: decent shaving utensils and post-shave lotion, non-greasy moisturiser, deodorant, lip balm and a face wash. Shower gel will be provided by any decent hotel, but it's still better to take your own, unless you relish the prospect of smelling like everyone else in the building.

## 04
### SHIRT, SHOWER AND SHAVE

Make time for a shower and a shave when you land. Ideally you'll have time to check into your hotel and shower before your first meeting, but if you don't, consider taking a quarter of an hour to shower at the airport. Pulling on a fresh shirt and (finally) grabbing a coffee will give you just the bounce you need.

05

## TAKE A MINUTE TO UNPACK

It's the last thing you'll feel like doing when you finally get to the hotel, but getting your clothes out of your suitcase and hanging them up as soon as you can will minimise crumpling. Should the damage be done, hanging them in the bathroom while you shower will help ease the creases out.

# THE KNACK

# HOW TO LOOK AFTER
# A CLASSIC CAR

*By Mr Michael Prichinello,*
*co-founder of the Classic Car Club, New York*

A CLASSIC CAR is different. Aside from its timeless cool and look, when you go through the gears of a vintage sports car, you feel them connecting and it's as if you are having a conversation with the car. They have an agricultural, mechanical feel that modern cars cannot match. Owning a classic car speaks volumes about your aesthetic and taste. If you were to drive a modern Ferrari, essentially what it says about you is that you have great credit. To own a Ferrari 308, or a Dino 246, says more about you as a person. It indicates you have panache. You're a risk-taker and willing to accept the responsibilities of a classic car, even if it means you can never be 100% sure you'll get to your destination in one piece or on time. If you look after them, you'll be repaid with a greater driving experience. Here are my tips for getting the old lady down the road safely.

## DO YOUR HOMEWORK

Take the time to read a couple of books that explain the main systems of combustion motors. For older cars to work you need a spark, you need fuel and you need air, and if you have a basic grasp of how those three systems work in a car, you'll be much more useful on the side of the road.

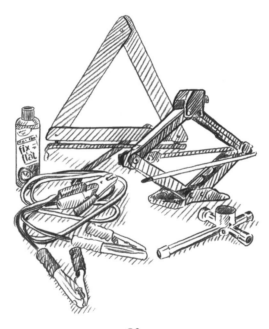

02

## ESSENTIAL KIT

With a good roadside tool kit you will get yourself out of most problems. This should include a jack, a can of tyre sealer (I use Fix-A-Flat), a wrench that matches your lug nuts, a triangle so people know to avoid you, and jumper cables. Jumper cables are the most important piece, because in classic cars the wiring gets old, which drains your battery.

## 03

### JOIN THE COMMUNITY

There are probably 30 or more online message boards dedicated to any particular car, whether you are a Ferrari guy, a Porsche guy or the owner of the most obscure car you can think of – someone out there will share your enthusiasm. I sign up and print off questions and answers and put them in a binder so that I have it with me in case I run into a situation or want to make an upgrade. There is an amazing community around classic cars, so make use of it.

## 04

### LOTIONS AND POTIONS

You need to invest in a good set of lotions and cleaning products – think of it like putting sunscreen on. I use Meguiar's products. One of the first things I do with a classic car is look at the sun visors – they are the first things to show a car's age. Use a good collection of Meguiar's a couple of times a year on the dash, the vinyl and the leather to keep the moisture in and they will stay nice.

## THE SECRET INGREDIENT

Old cars were made to run on gasoline containing lead, which is a really good lubricator. Modern gasolines don't contain any lead and have a lot of alcohol, which burns out the gaskets and other parts. It's good to put a can of Marvel Mystery Oil in with your petrol every now and then – it helps give natural minerals back to all the rubber portions of the motor and keeps everything fresh, sealed and tight.

06

### EVERY LITTLE HELPS

If you keep up on the little things, wear and tear won't spread like a rash. Rims, for example, are particularly important. They are what make a good car look great or a great car look poor. Find a local guy who refurbishes them – it's not expensive. On a lot of the old cars it's just highly polished aluminium.

# MR PRICHINELLO'S TOP THREE
## CLASSIC CARS

### TRACK-READY 1974 PORSCHE 911 MFI

A beautiful car in our fleet that we have modernised but kept
very period-correct

### 1969 JAGUAR E-TYPE

The quintessential classic car. Enzo Ferrari said it's the only car
that he wished had come off his assembly line

### 1969 FORD BRONCO

Classic cars don't always have to be beautiful saloons. I think
vintage trucks are awesome. The Bronco will tackle anything

# HOW TO PULL OFF
# DARING STUNTS

*Mr Vic Armstrong, the man behind the stunts for 007
and* Indiana Jones, *tells us how it's done*

HOW MANY MOVIES have you seen starring Mr Vic Armstrong? None? Think again. His name may not appear on opening credits or billboards, but as one of the world's leading stuntmen for the past four decades, Mr Armstrong, has planned and executed stunts (or "gags" as they are known in the business) for a list of movies that reads like a roll call of Hollywood's greatest action hits. Mr Harrison Ford's stunt-double in the *Indiana Jones* films? Step forward Mr Armstrong. Mr Gregory Peck's double in *Arabesque*, Mr George Lazenby's in *On Her Majesty's Secret Service*, Sir Roger Moore's in *Live and Let Die* and Mr Christopher Reeve's in the original *Superman* trilogy? Mr Armstrong is the man. And that's not to mention his key roles in *Blade Runner, Star Wars: Episode VI* and *Never Say*

*Never Again*, in the latter of which he performed stunts for Sir Sean Connery's Bond. More recently, Mr Armstrong has turned his hand to coordinating stunts and working as a second unit director on blockbusters including *Thor, Mission: Impossible III, War of the Worlds, Die Another Day, The World is Not Enough*, and, in a rare departure to a less masculine world, *Charlie's Angels*. ("Cameron Diaz was amazing," Mr Armstrong says. "She liked to come and hang out with the stuntmen.") Herewith are Mr Armstrong's tips:

OI

GET CREATIVE

The biggest stunt you do is coming up with something original. You either have a stunt specified in the script which is not impro vised during filming, or the script gives an outline and you work it out from there. For instance, all the script said for the boat chase in *Die Another Day* was "Bond leaves MI6 in a boat then ends up at the Millennium Dome" and they wanted a hot air balloon involved, so I drove up and down the Thames and dreamt up ideas. Locations give you the inspiration and ideas for thing.

## PLANNING MAKES PERFECT (ALMOST)

The key to staying safe is preparation. It's not balls to the wall, take a deep breath and hope it works; everything is calculated, partly because you want to work again – if you're injured, you're not getting paid. Once you have come up with your sequence, you say "OK, how are we going to do this" and you break down how it can be shot. It has to be dissected into steps that cover every detail, working with other departments such as set builders and special effects guys. Months of work can go into a sequence which is just a few seconds long, to make the result look as effortless as possible.

## 03
### PREPARATION

You don't need to psyche yourself up too much before performing a stunt, because so much preparation will have taken place beforehand, and you will be operating within an area which is your forte. In a movie there could be five stuntmen all doubling the same actor, each specialising in a field, be that driving, parkour, martial arts or horse riding. I wouldn't do anything if I thought it was too dangerous. That said, fire is one of the things I get nervous about because it is so instant and so final. It doesn't take any prisoners. High falls are the same: once you're in motion there is nothing you can do to stop… if it goes wrong you just land and break your neck.

## 04
### NO REGRETS AND NO DISTRACTIONS

I did a 100ft fall off a viaduct on *The Final Conflict*, and the night before I was thinking "What am I doing this for, this is crazy." The biggest fear any stuntman should have is that of failure. There are many variables in play and perhaps £250,000 worth of set that will be destroyed if there's an explosion involved. If you screw up, all that has to be rebuilt, so the responsibilities are immense. If an actor messes up his lines the scene can be repeated as many times as necessary. It's very different for us stuntmen when you get in front of the camera. You have to keep a level head.

# BE BETTER THAN A COMPUTER

Like morphine, CGI is an incredible thing used in the right quantities for the right reasons, but, if abused, it is a killer. In the old days on *Superman* we used to fly on single strand wires the same as you have in the piano, and if they snap, bang! They're gone and you hit the concrete. And we couldn't hide impact pads either, everything had to be painted out or hidden behind something, but now you can use wire as thick as your finger and it can be erased in post-production. You can have ramps and safety mats in the frame too and remove them later. So CGI can be a wonderful tool, but some directors create whole sequences using it. I think that is a disaster – the result looks fake and unrealistic – so we have to strive continually to be the best.

# HOW TO REVIVE OLD SHOES

*By Mr Costas Xenophontos of London's
legendary Classic Shoe Repairs*

A GOOD PAIR of shoes is often described as "an investment", but unlike most investments this is one that you put your feet into and then hit repeatedly against the ground. Small wonder, then, that even the best-made pairs can end up looking sub-prime. Having said that, a pair of lovingly worn old Oxfords says something about a man that box-fresh sneakers never could. But you'd best come to terms with the universal truth that all shoes, however treasured, must age. Don't forget that there are steps you can take to revive even the most beaten-up pair. One man who knows more about this than most is Mr Costas Xenophontos, director of Classic Shoe Repairs. His London workshop was founded in 1963 and has built a reputation as the finest cobbler in the city, entrusted with repairing worn and damaged shoes from some of the world's best designers.

## 01
### KNOW YOUR MATERIAL

Before treating your shoes, work out what they're made of. Leather comes in many forms: calf, nubuck, suede, goatskin, crocodile, alligator; some are made for everyday use and some are more delicate; the finish can be distressed or polished to a shine. There's a product for everything (I use products from Woly), so there's no need to settle for a generic polish. Just make sure you don't use the wrong one.

## 02
### NO STAIN NO GAIN

There are some stains that can't be completely shifted. The worst are hot oils, such as candlewax and cooking oil – especially on suede or nubuck, where the oil can remove the top layer of the leather. Watermarks, especially from salty, gritted pavements, are also difficult to remove. Don't expect to eradicate these completely – even dyeing your shoes won't get rid of them. And trying too hard will make it look worse.

## 03
### CALL IN THE PROFESSIONALS

It depends on how handy you are, but in general the best analogy is to treat your shoes like you treat your skin. Cleaning, polishing and applying treatments and creams are all things you can do at home. But when it comes to anything involving a knife, or a needle and thread, leave it to the experts. You wouldn't attempt amateur cosmetic surgery; the same should be true of your shoes.

## 04
### WHEN TO CALL IT A DAY

We see a lot of "vintage pieces" that people buy cheaply in the hope of fixing up. If you see a pair of shabby crocodile loafers in a second-hand store, don't assume they'll be restorable. If the surface of the leather has dried and cracked, it's time to throw them away. Leather needs nourishing and feeding – if it has been neglected for too long, there's no saving it. Sometimes you just have to let go.

## PREVENTATIVE CARE

Having grown up in the business, I've always been told to use shoe-trees (although I don't always practice what I preach). Put them in right after taking off your shoes, while they're warm and before the leather relaxes. Remember to occasionally treat the leather, too – a nourishing cream will keep it from drying. While these aren't tips on reviving shoes, they will keep you from having to take drastic measures later on.

## SOME COMMON MISTAKES

### DRYING SHOES ON THE RADIATOR

This is a great way to ruin your shoes, making the leather brittle and causing it to crack. If they're really drenched, stuff them with absorbent material – newspaper works well – and let them dry naturally.

### USING SUPERGLUE

A tempting option, but it's the worst stuff for leather. It's impossible to take it off without damaging the surface underneath, and if a shoe needs stitching the needle won't be able to pierce it.

### EXPENSIVE SHOES, BUDGET SHOE CARE

Your average high-street cobbler might not be used to handling classic, handmade shoes on a regular basis. It's worth the expense to avoid the risk of seeing your favourite pair come back to you with a cheap plastic heel, or worse.

# HOW TO THROW A GREAT PARTY

*By Mr Robin Scott-Lawson,*
*founder of events agency My Beautiful City*

"PARTY AT MY place?" is an offer that is all too easy to make, but one that can lead to disappointment, embarrassment and, if it is not followed through properly, social suicide. Luckily this need not be the case, because with a little thought and forward planning your parties can take off seamlessly, leaving you with the enviable reputation as the host with the most. We believe Mr Robin Scott-Lawson is the perfect man to offer a tip or two on holding great social gatherings, since his creative agency masterminds parties, fashion shows and film premieres for a long list of prestigious clients including Claridge's hotel and Ralph Lauren.

## 01
### PLANNING

When I'm throwing a party at my house I like to start with a theme.
Some might cringe at the idea, but the fact is it creates an atmosphere and gives you a point to start from. It's also a great talking
point, as deep down people love to get dressed up – plus you can
have fun with the interior of your house as well as linking the
theme to the food and drink.

## 02
### INVITATIONS

When it comes to invitations, one thing I've learnt from previous
parties is to draw up a list of only the people you want there – not
people you feel as if you have to invite. Make sure there are a few
mad characters included, to spice things up a bit and take the other
guests out of their comfort zones.

## 03
### AMBIANCE

I am obsessed with lighting. I think it is very important to people's moods and the general feel of a party. Keep it low and sexy. Never turn the lights up at the end of a party – very unfriendly. It's not closing time at the pub. One thing I like to do is use red-coloured light bulbs because they create this great underground bar feel. Decorations are key, but don't bother spending big on them, as you'll either chuck them out or they will get broken.

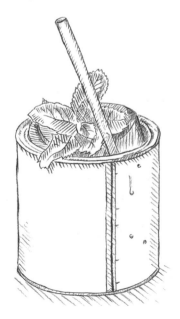

## 04
### SNACKS AND LIBATIONS

It's very important to make an effort and have fun with food and drink; it's something people will always remember and talk about afterwards. Little details can go a long way, so try out something new. For example, I once turned my house into a Western dive bar. As guests arrived, I served them whiskey and pickle juice in old paint jars. Another year we made little gingerbread men decorated to look like the guests at the party.

## 05
### PARTY TIME

Don't peak too early, get the music flowing and, most importantly, relax. It's no fun being the host who doesn't enjoy their own party, instead fretting too much about red wine spillages or the circulation of the canapés. I love a few pets at a party – my springer spaniel Charlie Murphy is always mingling, giving the guests strange looks of concern. And finally, get a cleaner booked for the next day, even if you have to pay a surcharge. That way you can hide under your duvet until order is restored.

# SOME COMMON MISTAKES

## RUNNING DRY

Run out of alcohol, and the fun will go with it. Ensure your bar (including non-alcoholic options for designated drivers) won't dry up by not being miserly with your purchasing, and also asking people to bring a bottle of something if necessary.

## INVITING TOO FEW

Is that the sound of tumbleweed rolling in? Unless you're planning a small, intimate get together, inviting too few people can lead to awkward situations. Don't assume that people will turn up, it's worth taking the time to check with them if they haven't RSVP'd.

## INVITING TOO MANY

Conversely, cramming people into your space like tinned sardines is never a good idea. Know the limits of your residence and consider hiring a venue if you are planning a mega bash. On a similar note, if your party will be very busy, keep an eye out for uninvited guests who heard the music from the street and let themselves in.

## CARELESS CANDLE POSITIONING

Although a sea of candles at floor level might seem like a good idea, an emergency visit from the fire department tends to kill the vibe. When the alcohol is flowing, naked flames are best avoided.

## INVITING SWORN ENEMIES

Whether your party is large or small, drawing up the guest list always requires a degree of diplomacy. You don't want to end up with the wrong sort of fireworks going off.

# HOW TO LACE YOUR NEW BOOTS

*By Mr Ian Fieggen (aka Professor Shoelace),*
*Melbourne, Australia*

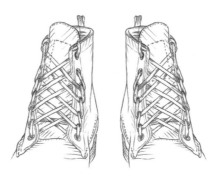

WINTER MEANS BOOTS, and lots of them. Boots can be worn for a host of different reasons; many are undoubtedly chosen for their utility, such as army boots or work boots, while it's the formality of others, such as dress boots or equestrian boots, which appeals. Meanwhile some, such as Diemme's hiking boots and Red Wing's biker boots, fill both these roles.

Just as there's a wide variety of boots, so there's a variety of ways to lace them. These can be selected for reasons of practicality or style; anything from unremarkable schemes that are worn purely for comfort, through to distinctive-looking patterns that will undoubtedly attract attention. A well-executed lacing pattern is the important finishing touch to any pair of boots, and indeed your outfit. We illustrate five contrasting techniques, some of which only you will appreciate, and some of which are likely to start some conversations.

## THE FAIL-SAFE

Most people (and most manufacturers) lace boots with
good old-fashioned criss-cross
lacing, and for good reason: it's
a simple, efficient method that
has stood the test of time. At
each pair of eyelets the shoelace ends cross each other and
feed under the sides and out
through the next higher pair
of eyelets. A no-brainer.

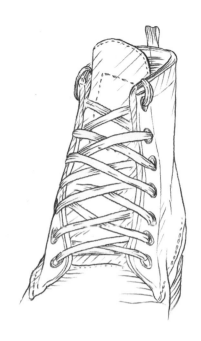

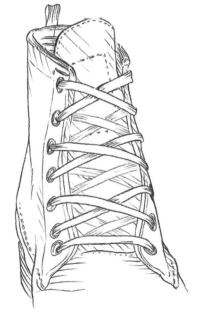

02

## FRICTION-FREE

My own preferred variation
is "over-under lacing", which
alternates between crossovers
on the inside and outside of
the boot. This reduces fric-
tion because the shoelaces
don't rub across the edges
of the boot, making it faster
and easier to pull only every
second crossover to tighten
or loosen. It's also easier to
get fingers underneath those
outer crossovers.

## 03
### ARMY APPROVED

Many armed forces (British, Dutch, French and Brazilian) lace their combat boots with "army lacing". At each pair of eyelets the shoelace ends cross each other on the inside of the boot, then run straight up the sides on the outside of the boot to the next higher eyelet pair. This allows the tough leather sides of the boots to flex more easily because they are not restricted by the crossovers (which are on the inside).

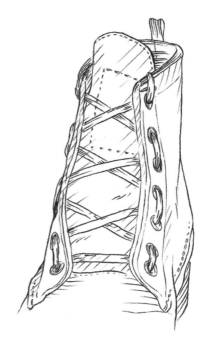

## 04
### THE LADDER

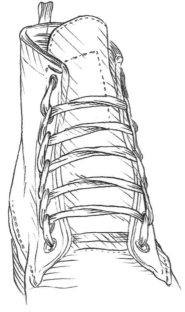

US paratroopers wear "ladder lacing" because it's a firm, secure style. It looks good on boots with lots of eyelets. Form a vertical section on each side between the bottom and second-from-bottom eyelets. At each eyelet pair, run the ends under the verticals on the opposite side before continuing up to the next higher eyelet pair. The end result resembles a straight ladder.

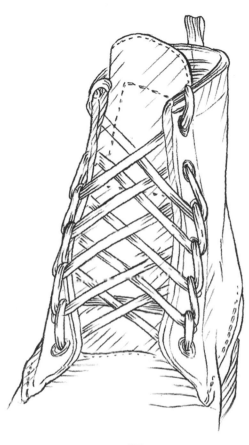

## 05

### CHARLOTTE'S WEB

"Spiderweb lacing" is not for the faint of heart. Start by forming a vertical section on each side, running down from the second-from-bottom eyelets to the bottom eyelets. Cross the ends and run diagonally up and out through the next pair. At each pair, run the ends down and under the verticals below before continuing diagonally up. With white shoelaces against black boots, this really lives up to its name, though it will mostly catch people's eyes instead of insects.

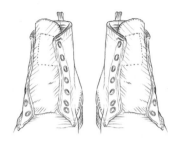

## 01

To avoid a messy result, try to be consistent with crossovers.
Either always cross left over right, or always right over left,
or always alternate.

## 02

For a symmetrical look, reverse the crossovers on the other boot.

## 03

When tying, avoid a "granny knot" or "slip knot", which both
sit crooked and come undone. A correctly tied shoelace knot
should sit straight across the boot and stay secure.

## 04

Better still, learn one of the many secure shoelace knots, which
will survive any boot-related punishment, whether you're out
hiking, or riding your motorbike.

## 05

Different lacing methods will require different lace styles
and lengths.

# HOT CHIP

*Our favourite left-field pop group's guitarist
and synth player, Mr Owen Clarke,
reveals what's on his iPod*

### "Hail Bop"
#### DJANGO DJANGO

"We keep bumping into these guys. We saw them in an American embassy and at several festivals, and we're touring with them in the UK. I like the guitars in this track – they sound Brian Eno-produced, sort of de-tuned, with a very electronic production."

### "Behind the Mask"
#### YELLOW MAGIC ORCHESTRA

"This track's been covered by Eric Clapton and Michael Jackson, so it has a ghostly appeal. I was always attracted to YMO as they list all their equipment on their records, as well as how much it costs to ship."

### "It Takes a Muscle to Fall in Love"
#### SPECTRAL DISPLAY

"It's one of those four-day songs – you have to listen to it as soon as you wake up and you can't stop. I learnt that M.I.A. had done a version, however, and it took the edge off it."

"This Must Be the Place"

TALKING HEADS

"This was one of my favourite songs at university and it's still my favourite now. There's no touring musician who doesn't cry just a little bit when they hear this. It's one of those beautiful/ happy/ sad songs."

"White Car in Germany"

ASSOCIATES

"I first heard this on BBC Radio 6 Music and had to know what it was instantly. Once it was in my head I kept singing it, which was slightly serendipitous as we were in Germany at the time doing promo work."

# PEACOATS

*Collar popped and brass buttons flashing, we take a look
at why this nautical number is the perfect
winter warmer*

ALTHOUGH IT'S A BOLD ASSERTION, there is truth in the statement that no man looks bad in the right peacoat. With its military origins, flattering cut and balanced design, this style of coat is a dependable wardrobe classic that has remained in fashion for decades – and is unlikely to go anywhere soon.

Pictured in the 1975 movie *Three Days of the Condor*, Mr Robert Redford
wore a sharp peacoat throughout

The first recorded mention of a peacoat in the *Oxford English Dictionary* dates back to 1717, so it's safe to say this style of double-breasted wool coat has a long history. There are several accounts of how the peacoat got its name. Among the most plausible are that the word is derived from the Dutch *pijjekker* (referring to a coarse-wool garment that labourers wore in the 18th century) or that it is a deviation of "P-jacket", an old military term for the type of jacket worn by a ship's pilot, or navigator.

A paradigm of Gallic style, Mr Serge Gainsbourg is seen here in Paris in the 1960s wearing a peacoat in place of a blazer over a shirt and tie

The terms "reefer jacket" and "officer's coat" are sometimes used to refer to the peacoat, affirming its naval origins. Modern peacoats, which are double breasted, cut short in the body and with broad collars, are derived from coats issued to US Navy personnel in the 1940s. These were based on the longer wool coats that British sailors had worn since the 1850s. Features such as the double set of buttons spaced apart (which were less likely to get caught in ropes on a ship) and the high collar to keep out the elements also hint at the peacoat's maritime heritage.

Unlike double-breasted blazers, which generally look best worn buttoned-up, the peacoat can look good worn unbuttoned too, thanks to the way it hangs. That said, there is something pleasing about wearing a peacoat fastened all the way to the top, as it brings to mind the sense of polished military style and good posture which is synonymous with its naval background. Continuing the seafaring theme, a striped Breton top is always a good partner to a peacoat – forget the peaked cap, though, unless you're going to a fancy-dress party.

In Paris, a peacoat worn with a button-down shirt, a crew-neck knit, slim navy jeans and suede desert boots is something of an autumn and winter uniform among stylish guys, and it's not difficult to see why. The key to getting this look right is to ensure that everything fits well and is cut fairly close to the body: oversized peacoats can dwarf you, so you should think rakish, not wrinkled, and streamlined, not saggy. Of course riding a moped while smoking, with a Ms Lou Doillon type perched behind, doesn't hurt in achieving the Parisian look either.

The peacoat falls somewhere between smart and casual, but generally speaking it is best not worn over a suit or for formal occasions. It can, however, be an excellent cold weather alternative to a suit jacket or blazer when teamed with tailored trousers and a shirt and knitted tie, while it can be easily dressed down with a T-shirt, jeans and sneakers. What's more, all types of knitwear go with peacoats (other than double-breasted cardigans – you don't want to overdo the DB), as do wool and corduroy trousers, and even chinos.

Mr Gregory Peck in *The Million Pound Note*, 1953

# MS MEGHAN MARKLE

*The sultry star of hit TV show* Suits *has definitely caught our eye. Here, we find out what catches hers*

AS WELL AS ticking all our sartorial boxes, legal drama *Suits* has provided us with our latest crush. Los Angeles-born actress Ms Meghan Markle is perhaps best known for her roles on *Fringe* and *CSI*, as well as a silver-screen appearance in *Horrible Bosses*, however it's her part as the cat-eyed, feisty-but-feminine paralegal Rachel Zane that has us hot under the collar. Here, Ms Markle gives us the nod on what she likes a man to wear, as well as the tips and tricks to get her attention – not that it will do you any good: sadly, someone already beat us to it.

*Your character, Rachel, is often asked for sartorial advice from Mike – is this something you are happy to dish out in real life?*
I think women have a really good sense of what looks good on men, especially if it's their own man, and in turn he should want to look good for her.

*Do you find yourself dressing your husband?*
He always wants a style makeover, and I'm not the best at it if I'm honest, but I try to piece things together for him. More than anything I think men look best when they dress simply, in a clean and sexy way – even if that's just a button-down shirt.

*What five things should every man have in his wardrobe?*
Definitely a beautifully tailored suit, and a perfect white button-down – which can be paired with something simple such as jeans or slacks, but always look fantastic. My husband wears basic black crew-neck T-shirts, which are very simple but oh-so-sexy; I happen to love a man in a linen shirt, it just makes me think of vacations and walking barefoot on the beach – and who doesn't like to think of that? And of course they need jeans. I also happen to love men in boat shoes, so I'd have to throw those in, too.

*Describe your perfect date from start to finish.*
A perfect date could be any number of things, but what's most important is that they are good company. It doesn't matter if it's fancy or not, it's all about the company and embracing every little second of it. I've had dates at the nicest restaurants, but when you leave you're starving and the best part of the date is having a slice of pizza and a couple of drinks on the way home. I think it's important to be able to roll with the punches and enjoy every minute of it. If he makes you laugh that helps.

*What is the best thing about playing Rachel Zane?*
The character of Rachel is so well written. She's strong, interesting and a little sassy, which I appreciate, and I love that she's still striving for something. Her ambition is something I find very attractive, so playing her is a lot of fun. I like that I not only get to play a romantic interest, but also a woman who is on the brink of a big career change.

*Who is the better dresser in your eyes, Harvey or Mike?*
It's so hard to choose. Harvey wears the most beautiful, perfectly tailored suits and he looks fantastic wearing them, but what I like about how Mike dresses is that he too wears beautifully tailored suits, but there is always a little bit of edge that keeps it from being perfect, and I find there's something very sexy about imperfection.

*What sort of suit gets your approval and why?*
I think a man in a suit always looks fantastic, but the other day the guys were wearing tuxedos on set and I had a moment where I did a double take and thought, "Oh my God, you guys look so hot." I think seeing a guy dressed up when you're not used to seeing someone that way is a big turn on.

*What should a guy buy a girl these days to impress her?*
For me it's never about the gift, rather than the thought behind it. I've been given extravagant gifts, but I think the things that always mean the most to me are those that are thoughtful, small and sweet. Although it's always nice to receive lingerie, but I guess that can be considered small and sweet, too.

*What is the best way to get your attention?*
It sounds so simple, but it's just to be kind. I think when you watch a man who is kind to whoever he is speaking with and you can see he is a good egg, it is the most attractive thing in the world. From there you get to know them and see their character, humour and ambition come through, but I still think kindness is the most important thing. That and being comfortable in your own skin.

*You are from LA but work in New York – which city's men are the better dressed?*
I have to apologise to my Californian natives, but I was just in New York and the sense of style there is overwhelming and so cool. I think the way people dress in that city is incredibly inspiring. Though I love the flip-flop culture of LA and I'm a true California girl at heart, there's nothing like getting dolled up in New York, with a sharply dressed man on your arm.

# THE REPORT
# ROCK OF AGES

*A closer look at history's most iconic guitars
and the men that made them famous*

THIS IS NOT a list of the world's finest guitarists (although that said, many happen to be on here), nor is it a guide to the world's best guitars. It is, rather, an appreciation of the musicians who, whether through chance or choice, have become synonymous with their guitar.

"Lucille is real, when I play her it's almost like hearing words, and naturally I hear cries," wrote Mr BB King in the liner notes of his 1968 album, *Lucille*. The blues musician's love affair with his guitar began after he ran into a burning club in 1949 to rescue his Gibson Archtop. On discovering the fire was caused by two men fighting over a woman whose name was Lucille, he named his guitar (and all subsequent models) after her to remind himself never to do anything so stupid. Whether he meant running into a burning building or fighting over a woman is unclear. You can now buy a Gibson 335 Lucille. The unique sound of the model is a by-product of its construction. Unlike other hollow-bodied guitars of the 1950s the 335 had a solid block of wood running through the centre, giving it the dark tone of a hollow body but the volume and control of a Les Paul.

Mr King, 1969

There have been countless legendary "Strats" since its inception in 1954, the versatile tone it produces being the backbone of recordings. From Mr Stevie Ray Vaughan's beaten 1963 Sunburst to Mr Eric Clapton's "Blackie", the used and abused Stratocaster holds a fascination for guitarists, the perception being that the more dents and dings, the better the player. Never was there a more road-weary guitar than Mr Rory Gallagher's infamous axe. It endured years of blood, sweat, cracks, crashes and modifications, and while Mr BB King has had several Lucilles, Mr Gallagher only ever had one Strat

Mr Gallagher, 1979

– and it showed. The finish proved no match for the guitarist's toxic sweat – the neck had to be retired due to damage and moisture-induced wood warping. When Mr Jimi Hendrix was asked what it was like to be the world's greatest guitar player, he replied, "Ask Rory Gallagher".

## MR BRIAN MAY'S "FIREPLACE"

The origin of Mr Brian May's home-built guitar has been documented many times in the music press, yet the story is worth repeating. Short of the necessary funds to purchase a new guitar at the start of his career, Mr May and his father decided to build one. The result was an instrument that was utterly unique. The body and neck were fashioned from a 200-year-old oak fireplace (complete with token wormholes) and copious coats of Rustin's plastic coat

Mr May, 1978

furniture polish that gave the guitar its distinctive red hue. If that wasn't inventive enough, the tremolo system was made from a knife, two motorcycle valve springs and a knitting needle tip. Needless to say, after 40 years on the road the "Red Special" was in serious need of repair and was handed to Australian guitar luthier Mr Greg Fryer, who rebuilt the instrument as well as three replicas, two of which Mr May uses to this day.

## MR BRUCE SPRINGSTEEN'S
### FENDER ESQUIRE/TELECASTER

Mr Springsteen, 1984

Slung casually around his neck, the Fender Esquire took pride of place on the cover of Mr Springsteen's third album, *Born to Run*. While the New Jersey-born rock singer isn't perceived as the greatest guitar picker to have wielded Fender's first electric design (Mr Springsteen considers Mr Jeff Beck to hold that honour), it has become as much a part of his working man persona as blue jeans and sleeveless shirts. According to Mr Springsteen, the guitar is the "bastard", the body taken from an early Telecaster, the neck from an Esquire. The tuning pegs and scratch plate have been changed, while its sports features come from models between 1953 and 1957. Bought sometime in the early 1970s from a luthier in his hometown, Mr Springsteen has now retired his faithful companion, which currently resides in the Rock and Roll Hall of Fame in Ohio.

## MR EDDIE VAN HALEN'S "FRANKENSTRAT"

When Mr Van Halen's eponymous debut record appeared in 1978, no one had seen or heard anything like it. The lead singer's signature "two hands on the neck" approach to the guitar gave his soloing a recognisable sound. His guitar of choice was as unusual as his style, and it was built to suit his preferences. Boogie Bodies (a company that built replacement parts for Fender) supplied the body and neck, while the Gibson pickup was wired by Mr Van Halen and mounted to the body along with a Stratocaster tremolo. The Frankenstrat hybrid was born. It was modified as things wore out or failed, and sometimes because the Dutch-born guitarist loved to misdirect those who tried to copy him. Many replicas have been constructed, mostly without Mr Van Halen's approval, although authorised tribute models with cigarette burns, "rattle can" paint and an inflated price tag are available.

Mr Van Halen, 1979

After a spell playing with Mr John Mayall (replacing Mr Clapton in the Bluesbreakers in 1966), Mr Green formed Fleetwood Mac. His main guitar through that period was his 1959 Les Paul, which has been the subject of discussion for some 40 years. How did he achieve that tone, so different from other guitars? Many explanations were put forward, suggesting the instrument was rewired incorrectly after a service or the tone pots were changed, or that the pickups were fitted backwards. The truth emerged after Mr Green sold the guitar to Mr Gary Moore. Mr Moore dismantled it and discovered no such wiring. In fact, the polarity on one pickup was reversed, suggesting the guitar was a factory defect. The chances of such a unique guitar ending up in the hands of such a unique player are staggering, equally the fact that it was rumoured to have been sold for $1.2m in 2006.

Mr Green, late 1970s

Modern stadium rock music owes its origins to this guitarist and his unique approach. His musical style and sound has influenced a generation of players, so much so that even The Edge himself feels there is a degree of self-parody when he straps on that guitar. Beloved of 1970s metal and glam rock bands, the Explorer's outrageous look suggest it was beamed down from space rather than built by craftsmen in Kalamazoo, Michigan. Bought in a New York guitar store by the U2 guitarist when he was 17, it was with serious apprehension that he debuted the guitar with the rest of the band. After initial jibes and sideways looks, the guitar became as recognisable as the band itself. It survived an altercation in Radio City Music Hall in New York, when the headstock was snapped off, and although his Explorer was apparently auctioned for charity, it remains unclear if that was the original model.

The Edge, 1979

The SG was designed by Gibson as part of the Les Paul model range, which goes some way to explain why the early models had the Les Paul signature logo on the headstock. However the SG was not to Mr Les Paul's taste and he demanded his name be removed from future versions. Much lighter and with a slimmer, faster neck which allowed easier access to the higher frets, it was well ahead of its time. For a small-handed Mr Angus Young, the slim neck was an attractive feature. His first SG (allegedly a '67) became so damaged with moisture ingress (read: sweat) that it had to be replaced. Little wonder given the musician's onstage antics. Whether sprinting across the stage, vaulting from the drum riser or faking a spasm on the floor (allegedly done the first time to avoid embarrassment at tripping over his own lead) he never stands still, drenching himself and his guitar.

Mr Young, 1980

The "Trigger" was acquired in 1969 and named after cowboy actor Mr Roy Rogers' horse, and the 78-year-old musician has never appeared on stage without it. Trigger is nylon rather than steel strung, which gives it a softer, mellower tone despite Mr Willie Nelson's intense flatpicking style. The guitar has signatures from more than 100 friends and colleagues including the late Mr Johnny Cash and Mr Waylon Jennings. In addition, Mr Nelson's picking has worn a hole through the top of the guitar. In 1990 the Internal Revenue Service (IRS) claimed Mr Nelson owed an astronomical $32m in taxes and subsequently many of his assets were auctioned off. It was Trigger that he feared losing the most, having once saved it from his burning home, stating: "When Trigger goes, I'll quit." Fortunately, he hid the guitar at his manager's house, depriving the IRS of the satisfaction of selling it to the highest bidder.

Mr Nelson, 2009

To list Sir Paul McCartney's achievements would be impossible given his huge influence not only on songwriting but the whole of popular culture. However, in 1961 Sir Paul bought his first Höfner 500/1, or "violin bass" as it became known. Unable to afford the Fender that he wanted, he bought the Höfner on the premise that it was symmetrical and would look less odd being played left-handed. Höfner was a small company, so was delighted when The Beatles gained momentum, and consequently gave Sir Paul his second Höfner in 1963 to use at the *Royal Variety Performance*. It's this guitar that has stayed with him throughout his career (the first was stolen) and despite being unused through much of the 1970s and early 1980s, Sir Paul was persuaded by Mr Elvis Costello to bring it out of retirement for the recording of *Flowers in the Dirt*, released in 1989.

Sir Paul, 1963

# MYSTERY JETS

*The lead singer of the indie outfit, Mr Blaine Harrison,
reveals his all-time top tracks*

### "What a Fool Believes"
#### THE DOOBIE BROTHERS

"The Doobies were a big influence on our new record, *Radlands*, and this song is a total country disco smash. When we were living out in Texas, pretty much all we listened to were cokey country records from the 1970s or whatever cab drivers would play us."

## "Birds"
### NEIL YOUNG

"I was a real latecomer to Neil Young because I had only heard his more rocky stadium stuff, which sounds kind of like Bon Jovi. 'Birds' always makes me feel like crying. He does a thing in the chorus where he skips a beat in the bar; you don't really notice it but it creates this subconscious tension."

## "I Drink"
### MARY GAUTHIER

"Something about this song reminds me of Marianne Faithfull, maybe the way her voice sounds like damaged goods. And there's great pedal steel on it. We have a pedal steel player touring with us – it's like this wash of colour that makes everything glow."

## "Follow Baby"
### PEACE

"These guys are from Birmingham and have supported us on tour. They're kind of like an old 1990s baggy band and are all shamefully talented and young. This track sounds like the Mondays crossed with Soundgarden."

## "I Found You"
### ALABAMA SHAKES

"I have been to see them play and they totally smashed it. They have all these songs that could be huge hits in some kind of parallel universe where the charts aren't full of David Guetta spin-offs and lame *X Factor* fodder."

## THE CLASSICS
# TWEED JACKETS

*This country staple has been revamped and now*
*looks as good worn in town on a date as*
*it does in a field on a tractor*

GIVEN THE RELAXED nature of modern dress codes, men's clothes must be versatile, and few items are as versatile as the tweed jacket, one of MR PORTER's fall essentials and one of 20 items we believe every man should own. Need to dress up for a client meeting? Put on a tweed jacket, a shirt and tie, a pair of grey wool trousers and some brown suede shoes. Going on a date? Put on a tweed jacket, a white T-shirt, a pair of slim jeans and some desert boots. Going for a walk in the country? Put on a tweed jacket, a flannel shirt, corduroy trousers and a pair of Wellington boots. You get the idea. Like a Land Rover, a robust tweed jacket can go almost anywhere, and like a Land Rover, a tweed jacket is a British design classic.

However, as for how to wear one in a contemporary manner, we suggest the American Ivy style. This look involves slim chinos, Oxford cloth or chambray button-down shirts, and brown loafers or desert boots.

The Duke of Windsor in New York, circa 1920s

The Duke of Windsor, a Prince of Wales from another era, reminds us of tweed's sporting origins, because back in the 1920s this would have been considered so casual it was only fit for the golf course or the horse track. That the Duke of Windsor dressed so casually on his trip to New York caused a controversy. Note the Duke's subtle sartorial idiosyncrasies: the two-button jacket on which both buttons are designed to be fastened, and the soft shoulders.

Mr Jean-Paul Belmondo and Ms Anna Karina in *Pierrot le Fou*, 1965

No man has ever looked as cool in a tweed jacket as Mr Jean-Paul Belmondo does in the French New Wave films of Mr Jean-Luc Godard. While the cut of Mr Belmondo's jackets might look a little loose these days, it's the nonchalance with which he wears them that's so appealing. The fact that he always seems to have a beautiful woman in tow is, we feel, testament to tweed's appeal.

Mr Sami Frey and Ms Brigitte Bardot, Paris, 1962

The French actor Mr Sami Frey, who's best remembered for his role in the 1964 Nouvelle Vague film *Band à Part*, proves that a tweed jacket is capable of giving a man an air of such consummate sophistication that it can be worn to squire the world's most beautiful woman around Paris. Mr Frey's smart outfit demonstrates how to dress for dinner, in a tweed jacket.

THE REPORT
# 10 ICONIC SUPERCARS

*In celebration of motoring craftsmanship,
we pick our most legendary drives*

### PORSCHE
### 911 Turbo

No supercar list would be complete without the Porsche 911. Essentially the same distinctively designed rear-engined machine created by Mr Ferdinand Porsche and unveiled by the Germans in 1963, over the years this curvaceous piece of perfection has been tweaked and improved – but at its heart it remains the same. Its legendary status was assured in 1974 when Porsche introduced the first turbocharged engine. Coupled with its muscular styling, gigantic spoiler and thrilling handling, it became a bona fide driving classic.

## BUGATTI
## Veyron 16.4

An engineering experiment that ultimately seemed to defy the laws of physics, the Bugatti Veyron – which debuted in 2005 – is a wonder of 21st-century technology. It is capable of more than 250mph. It can travel from 0–60mph in 2.5 seconds. And it has an 8-litre, 16-cylinder engine with four turbochargers producing 1,001bhp. Not everyone loves it, of course. McLaren F1 designer Mr Gordon Murray described its creation as "the most pointless exercise on the planet". But if God owned a supercar, it would be a Bugatti Veyron. And he wouldn't just drive it on Sundays, either.

## FERRARI
## F40

According to Mr Jeremy Clarkson, the Ferrari F40 is not just a supercar – it is *the* supercar. For a 25-year-old machine that the Italians put together in just 12 months to celebrate the company's 40th anniversary, that's quite an accolade. Ironically, in order to save weight the F40 was so stripped down and basic – no stereo, electric windows or proper door handles – that it felt and drove more like a racing car. And that was the whole point, making it the world's first road-legal car to hit a top speed of more than 200mph.

### MCLAREN
#### F1

In 1988 McLaren set about designing the greatest road car the world had ever seen. Four years later the F1 confirmed that, as a super-car creator, it was in a league of its own. With money no object (an

engine bay lined with gold foil, anyone?), it was the fastest production car ever built, the first to have a fully carbon fibre monocoque, and even offered a unique central driving position. And just to demonstrate how far ahead of the field it was, in 1998 it registered a top speed of 240mph. It remains the fastest naturally aspirated production car in the world.

## MERCEDES-BENZ
### 300SL

Not, strictly speaking, a true supercar, the 300SL makes our top 10 because of what it represents. Because in a list of cars that are almost all capable of hitting 200mph, the fact that the 300SL was the fastest production car of its day really doesn't mean that much… until you consider quite how fast 160mph was in 1954. An incredible achievement, but one rendered inconsequential by a design of such timeless beauty that it probably wouldn't matter if it didn't even move. The crowning glory of the 300SL remains the gullwing doors – one of the automotive world's most unforgettable silhouettes.

## LAMBORGHINI
### Miura

Created in 1966 by a small team of young engineers against the wishes of company owner (and tractor manufacturer) Mr Ferrucio Lamborghini, the result was a mid-engined piece of automotive artwork that redefined car design. From the dark headlight eyelashes and doors, which when open resembled the horns of a bull (inspiring the name), to the elegant rear that is as pert as that of Ms Raquel Welch's, the Miura was V12 sex on four wheels.

## FERRARI
### 250 GTO

For the 250 GTO, created in 1962 to compete on the GT racing circuit, Ferrari took the chassis of the 250 GT SWB, installed the 3-litre V12 engine from the Testa Rossa, and let designer Mr Sergio Scaglietti loose on a wooden frame with sheets of aluminium and a hammer. Consequently, each of the 39 GTOs were slightly different, or, as Ferrari enthusiasts will tell you, all the more perfect for their

imperfections. With the right racing pedigree, GTOs are currently changing hands for as much as £20m. And only for a car this stunning could that be considered a bargain.

PAGANI
Zonda

No one could ever accuse Mr Horacio Pagani of being subtle. When the former Lamborghini engineer set up his own carbon fibre-inspired supercar company, his aim was to create a car influenced

by the Sauber-Mercedes Silver Arrows and with the perfect mix of art and automotive science. The result, in 1999, was a unique, flame-spewing, wingless fighter plane that is able to compete with anything on four wheels. Aggressive, imposing, inspiring and out-rageous, it is a car capable of taking your breath away, then blowing your mind.

## FORD
## GT40

Back in the early 1960s, Mr Henry Ford II had a dream: he wanted one of his cars to race at Le Mans. So he went to the competition. He tried (and failed) to buy Ferrari, negotiated with Lotus, and ultimately recruited Lola designer Mr Eric Broadley. The result, unveiled in 1964, was the incredible GT40. So called because it was just 40 inches high at the windscreen, this V8 dream machine not only got Ford to Le Mans, it also ended Ferrari's stranglehold on the race, sweeping to four consecutive victories between 1966 and 1969. Thanks to its badge it was considered the people's supercar, and due to popular demand, in 2005 Ford brought it back from the dead in the (slightly taller) shape of the Ford GT.

## LAMBORGHINI
### Countach

For boys of a certain vintage, the 1974 Lamborghini Countach was their bedroom wall. But for them, the fact that such an astonishing slab of Italian automotive beauty actually existed in the real world didn't matter. What did matter was its mind-blowing scissor doors, its Mr Marcello Gandini-designed flying wedge shape, and the fact that its name, Countach, doesn't have a direct English translation. It was simply a regional Italian expression to describe one's astonishment at the looks of a gorgeous woman. (If it had been made in the UK, we would have called it the Lamborghini Crikey.)

# BIKER JACKETS

*Rugged and rebellious (grr!), the biker jacket
is an enduring wardrobe staple*

THERE'S SOMETHING ABOUT leather biker jackets: as soon as you slip one on, you instantly become a more rebellious, alive version of yourself, with the swagger to match – even if you're not a biker or rock star. It doesn't matter if the closest contact you have with a motorbike is when a courier delivers your online shopping; biker jackets are such a masculine and effortlessly stylish wardrobe staple, it's impossible to resist getting in on the action.

The biker jacket evolved from the leather jackets originally worn by drivers and pilots in the late 19th and early 20th century. These provided a shield against dust, grease and the weather (essential in the days when cars and cockpits were unenclosed), as well as some protection in the event of an accident. When the motorcycle came onto the scene, a jacket with similar properties was required for its riders, with the principal modification that it would be shorter in length than driving coats, and less bulky than leather flight jackets.

Mr Andy Warhol, pictured in New York City in 1968, was a fan of the
biker jacket. Here he wears one over a double-breasted blazer
for an idiosyncratic look

The distinctive double-breasted, zip-up style of biker jacket (commonly known as the Perfecto, and made famous by Mr Marlon Brando in the 1950s) was developed by Schott NYC. The Schott brothers pioneered their now-iconic jacket in 1928, and its design has changed very little since then. With a snug fit tailored to the body, broad lapels held in place by push-stud fasteners, and a diagonal zip, the Perfecto set an early benchmark for biker jacket design.

Mr Marlon Brando, seen here on the set of *The Wild One* in 1953, was largely responsible for elevating the biker jacket to the iconic status it enjoys today

Although they were born out of practicality, biker jackets soon became desirable for style purposes – and not just because of their flattering cut. In the 1950s teenage rebels adopted biker jackets, emulating the style and attitude of their screen heroes Messrs Marlon Brando and James Dean, leading schools to ban them. Since then, several style subcultures, from greasers to rockers to punks, have made biker jackets their own, attracted by the sense of rebellion and adventure that they convey.

The Sex Pistols' Mr Sid Vicious, photographed in London in 1978, drops the rebellious attitude that biker jackets call for

Since the mid-20th century, members of biker gangs have customised their jackets by adding pins and patches, or by painting designs and motifs onto the back of them. In the 1970s and 1980s, punk rockers mirrored this, beating up their jackets and adorning them with safety pins and metal studs. Even if you're not planning on customising yours, don't be afraid to let it get well-worn – biker jackets look best once they are broken in and have acquired some personality.

The easiest, most timeless way to wear a biker jacket is with jeans, a T-shirt and leather boots. This look can be amped up or toned down depending on whether you opt for a shredded T-shirt and tight black jeans, or a white crew neck and classic selvedge denims. The key to wearing a biker jacket well is to look as if you don't care. It should look as if it was slung on, rather than carefully selected, and as if you left it crumpled on your girlfriend's bedroom floor the night before, not kept on a padded hanger in a closet.

Since the biker jacket is an inherently casual item, loaded with a sense of adventure and rebellious spirit, it can be worn over a shirt and tie to create an interesting contrast or style tension. With the same principle in mind, consider wearing one over a tailored jacket or with tailored trousers (but not with both at the same time) for a contemporary look with an edge. Biker jackets go well with plaid too, since it picks up on the vintage US heritage which lies behind their design.

# ACKNOWLEDGEMENTS

Editor-in-Chief – Mr Jeremy Langmead
Art Director – Mr Leon St-Amour
Editor – Ms Jodie Harrison
Production Manager – Ms Xanthe Greenhill
Style Director – Mr Dan May
Designers – Messrs Eric Åhnebrink,
Rik Burgess, David Pearson
Picture Editor – Ms Katie Morgan
Editorial Assistant – Ms Caroline Hogan
Deputy Sub Editor – Mr James Coulson

## CONTRIBUTORS

Mr Angelo Trofa, Ms Cherry Imbush, Mr Chris Elvidge,
Mr Ian Tansley, Ms Iona Davies, Mr Jacopo Maria Cinti,
Mr Lewis Malpas, Mr Mansel Fletcher, Ms Marie Belmoh,
Mr Peter Henderson, Ms Rachael Smart, Mr Scott Stephenson,
Ms Sophie Hardcastle, Mr Tom M Ford, Mr Tony Cook

With immense thanks to:

Ms Natalie Massenet, without whom this book,
or company, wouldn't exist

# PHOTO CREDITS

THE LOOK: Mr Tinie Tempah – Angelo Pennetta

THE CLASSICS: Sweatshirts – Sunset Boulevard/Corbis, Writer Pictures, Peter Pakvis/Redferns/Getty Images

MEN OF NOTE: Road Tracks – Martyn Goddard/Corbis

THE LOOK: Mr Damian Lewis – Kurt Iswarienko

THE REPORT: Take Me Out – Moviestore Collection

THE INTERVIEW: Mr David Hockney – Tony Evans/Getty Images, Ed Kashi/Corbis

THE CLASSICS: The Shawl-Collar Cardigan – eyevine, Tony Frank/Sygma/Corbis, Wenn

MEN OF NOTE: Perfume Genius – Angel Ceballos

THE LOOK: Mr Hidetoshi Nakata – Angelo Pennetta, Stu Forster/Allsport/Getty Images

THE CLASSICS: The Bomber Jacket – W. Eugene Smith/Time & Life Pictures/Getty Images, John Springer Collection/Corbis, Rex Features

THE INTERVIEW: Mr Irvine Welsh – Scott Trindle

WOMEN OF NOTE: Sunday Girl – Billy Ballard

THE INTERVIEW: Mr John Pawson – Jamie Hawkesworth, Jens Weber

THE CLASSICS: Polo Shirts – eyevine, Marianne Rosenstiehl/Sygma/Corbis, Evening Standard/Getty Images

STYLE ICONS: © Pierre Fournier/Sygma/Corbis, Paul Popper/Popperfoto/Getty Images, Dezo Hoffmann/Rex Features,

Roger-Viollet/Rex Features, Rex Features, Slim Aarons/
Hulton Archive/Getty Images, Robin Platzer/Twin Images/
Time & Life Pictures/Getty Images , © Thomas Laisné/Corbis,
Apic/Getty Images, © Norman Parkinson/Sygma/Corbis,
Riama-Pathe/The Kobal Collection, © Michael Nicholson/
Corbis, © Dennis Stock/Magnum Photos, © Norman
Parkinson Ltd/Courtesy Norman Parkinson Archive, Slim
Aarons/Getty Images, Redux/eyevine, Vittorio Zunino
Celotto/Getty Images, Terry O'Neill/Getty Images, Cat's
Collection/Corbis, Jean-Louis Swiners/Gamma-Rapho/Getty
Images, Arnold Newman/Getty Images, Slim Aarons/Getty
Images, © CinemaPhoto/Corbis, Rex Features, © Lynn Gold-
smith/Corbis, Michael Ochs Archives/Getty Images, Anwar
Hussein/Hulton Archive/Getty Images, Everett Collection/
Rex Features, Mary Evans Picture Library/Hardy Amies
London, Popperfoto/Getty Images, Xposure Photos, Alan
Band/Keystone/Getty Images

MEN OF NOTE. Mr Matthew Dear    Will Calcutt
MEN OF NOTE: Grizzly Bear – John Lindquist
THE REPORT: Mr Charles Schumann – Christian Kain
THE LOOK: Mr Jason Sudeikis – Alexei Hay, Allstar Picture
    Library
MEN OF NOTE: Diplo – Shane McCauley
THE LOOK: Mr Vincent Kartheiser – Mr Kurt Iswarienko
THE CLASSICS: Knitted Ties – FilmMagic/Getty Images, ABC
    Photo Archives/Getty Images, Rex Features
ONES TO WATCH: Mr Allen Leech – Brendan Freeman
MEN OF NOTE: Hot Chip – Steve Gullick
THE CLASSICS: Peacoats – Ronald Grant Archive, Rex Features
THE CRUSH: Ms Meghan Markle – John Lindquist
THE REPORT: Rock of Ages – Michael Ochs Archives/Getty
    Images, Sunshine/Retna Pictures, Ed Perlstein/Redferns/

Getty Images, S Granitz/Getty Images, Getty Images, G AB Archive/Redferns/Getty Images, Paul Slattery/Retna Pictures, Michael Putland/Getty Images, Raoul F. Kassad/Retna Ltd./ Corbis, I TV/Rex Features

MEN OF NOTE: Mystery Jets – Henry Harrison

THE CLASSICS: Tweed Jackets – Rex Features, Kobal Collection, Agence France-Presse/Getty Images

THE CLASSICS: Biker Jackets – Santi Visalli Inc/Getty Images, Rex Features, Steve Emberton/Camera Press, London

# ILLUSTRATION CREDITS

THE KNACK: How to Appreciate Jazz – Mr Angelo Trofa
How to Behave in a Spa – Mr Angelo Trofa
How to Bond with your Father-in-Law – Mr Angelo Trofa
How to Dance at a Wedding – Mr Angelo Trofa
How to Create a Bespoke Bloody Mary – Mr Angelo Trofa
How to Dress for a Festival – Mr Angelo Trofa
How to Get out of a Hair Rut – Ms Anje Jager
How to Hit the Ground Running – Mr Joe McKendry
How to Look After a Classic Car – Ms Anje Jager
How to Pull off Daring Stunts – Mr Joe McKendry
How to Revive Old Shoes – Mr Angelo Trofa
How to Throw a Great Party – Mr Angelo Trofa
How to Lace Your New Boots – Mr Angelo Trofa

MR PORTER is the global online retail
destination for men's style,
offering more than 200 of the world's
leading menswear brands.